HOW TO SAY IT SO THEY HEAR IT

DAVID R. SHOWALTER

Illustrated by Roy Weier

©Copyright 1973 by Ann Arbor Science Publishers, Inc.
P.O. Box 1425, Ann Arbor, Michigan 48106

Library of Congress Catalog Card No. 72-96911
ISBN 0-250-40016-2
All Rights Reserved
Printed in the United States of America

David R. Showalter
(1915-1972)
PREFACE ...... APPRECIATION

Twice now I've read David Showalter's volume of genial but insistent advice on getting ourselves heard. The first reading was for curiosity, the second for delight revisited. Later readings will be for further enlightenment, more good sense, practical communications reminders, and always, for additional moments and morsels of frisky pleasure. This is going to be one of those books for repeat encounters, and as an incurable book accumulator with hundreds always waiting for attention, that is a reader's sincerest tribute.

In this instance it is also a professional tribute. As a long-time performer in the New York communication and corporation gymnasiums, from the pushups of a copywriter to the parallel bars of an advertising manager, I have read most books written to help businessmen cope with communications problems. Spanning more years than it takes to qualify for bar mitzvah, recognition as an Apache warrior, or four times the statute of limitations for most crimes, I have reread only one book on communications: This one.

What is the book's secret? I'll be darned if I know exactly, though I have theories. It is an impossible book to press into the neat confines of a tidy definition. A "how to" book on communications with sound directions for putting our points across, publicly or privately, and being *heard,* it is also a book of memoirs-reflections-truths, small and large, from a man whose broad professional career in the communications field included public relations director for **CBS** Radio and executive secretary for the motion picture and television committee of the National Safety Council.

Why not admit it is several books in one and get it over with. It approaches the over-jargoned, often tiresomely pedantic subject of modern communications in a special, personal, new, and compelling way. Mr. Showalter reminds us of things forgotten or teaches us things not known, and contrives somehow to make us like it. On my personal shelf of "specials," this book will join Gene Fowler's *Minutes of the Last Meeting,* Arnold Bennett's *How To Live on Twenty-Four Hours A Day* (critical dilemma in 1910), Sterne's' *Tristram Shandy,* Fred Allen's correspondence, and another dozen or so fascinating mavericks persistently too much for ordinary halters and conventional classifications.

". . . So They Hear It" is a guidebook-memoir-autobiography-lecture-sermon-soap box oration-graduate thesis of a working lifetime. It meanders with selective care through a gamut of communication areas involving many of the big and little shots of our epoch. It is concerned with a pushy general, film stars, television executives, one of the richest men in the world, seat-of-the-pants pilots, and even Gary Cooper's "Yep." The ostensible, comprehensive subject is the XYZ's of communication (the book is two alphabets beyond the ABC's). But in this considered product of a communicating life, David Showalter simultaneously tackles the ins and outs, the ways and sideways, of contemporary intercourse between and among humans. To a remarkable extent he gets away with it, and we learn while laughing.

As you read, don't forget this is a special book. It requires patience from a reader, and something more than an occasional appreciative yawn. It is the testament and experience of an exceptional man, and it doesn't obey the conventional rules. Deliberately I suspect. From the author's robust prose to Roy Weier's frivolously non-frivolous illustrations, it is clearly a work with neither time nor inclination to plow a straight and narrow furrow down the straight and narrow cornfield.

The author wasn't trying to perpetrate a textbook, and by not trying he may have succeeded rather ironically in doing just that for managers, engineers, executives, students, housewives, et al, literally everyone with an abiding interest in being heard.

I think David Showalter wanted to record in this permanent form the guts and brain insight he had learned through his years as an American communications practitioner. He wanted to help us get on our feet, and get it said, and get it heard, whatever our job, whether it is addressing colleagues at the factory, the office, the parole board, Congress, the United Nations, a local Boy Scout Troop, the Committee, the husband and/or wife with that glazed, non-listening look all of us know. This book makes it easier. The suggestions here are from the heart of a man who got it done, and from the mind of a man who learned how to do it. What more should we ask?

David Showalter learned how to say it simply and accurately without rhetorical embroidery: "Communication means getting somebody to do something for you." I don't know a better summary in fewer syllables. Ultimately that is the sole objective of communication whether the target is wife, boss, subordinate, or a sceptically listening traffic policeman. This book has useful hints concerning the dynamics and human participation factors of speaking-listening communications that *may* even contribute beneficially at such broken law moments, perhaps gain you a ticket rather than overnight in durance vile.

I'll make a deal with you. Read conscientiously to the account of the character actor and the three unforgettable Alaskan criteria for escaping greenhorndom. Page number withheld to discourage peeking. If by then you don't agree David Showalter has implemented a uniquely painless way to supply communications know-how, basic wisdom, and witty diversion, I'll pay the worst forfeit imaginable: I'll read every word including the index in any standard 700 page work you care to name on the arts of written and spoken communications, and I shall remain remorselessly sober while doing so.

It is a frightening forfeit I expect never to be demanded. When you reach the greenhorn segment, you'll be saying as I did, "This is the doggonedest, dadburnedest, most incisively insightful surveillance of communications ways, means, don't's and do's, ever melded together. Showalter says it so I can hear, and I shouldn't be surprised if I'm acquiring bits of the knack myself."

By then you'll agree from his writing style, his asides, his anecdotes, his reminiscences, the jauntiness of his method, that David Showalter in this book is assuredly one of the good companions.

He was one of those writing men with the gift of writing as if he were talking directly to you across a table or a mountaintop. There are many who can be scholarly, literary, logical, and neat. What's tough when facing an empty sheet of paper is to be human. David Showalter accomplishes his writing consistently in a bustling, straightforward, cranky, determined, sprightly human way.

To my regret, I never met David Showalter, but I know him well because of this book. I know him as if we had met and talked a hundred times, played poker together, or doodled side by side at media selection meetings and wondered what the *sane* people were doing. I suspect every meeting David Showalter attended was a little saner, and more productive, because he was there.

He was a get-it-done man, with compassion. The evidence is also here that he was a talking man, one of those good companions who "tired the sun with talking and sent it down the sky." I can imagine one of his friends, in laughing surrender as David Showalter sounded off on the communications bellyaches of the day, amiably advising: "Dave, get a soapbox." And I can imagine the author thinking it over and going to work. In this book, from a personal soapbox for an audience of you and me, he talks and tells stories and instructs and beguiles. Quite a lot of this talk will stay alive in your memory, and mine.

David Showalter was worth knowing, and he is worth remembering. He wasn't a word mincer or word waster. He faced facts without prejudice or tremor. He was an enemy of both humbug and the humdrum. He valued the individual, and the private, eccentric ways of individuals in our increasingly homogenized society of suffocating sameness. His head was awake and his eyes were open at a time when so many heads and eyes have seemed struthiously closed. Yes, he was worth knowing, and he is worth listening to: These words for example about change:

"Change is painful. Change is difficult to achieve. We are inclined to stay in an uncomfortable, uninhabitable rut rather than change to something new. We would rather be comfortable in our accustomed uncomfortableness than uncomfortable in an unaccustomed uncomfortableness."

Is this a word portrait of you, or me, or the status quo experts next door? I know this with conviction: It wasn't David Showalter. He wasn't a head-in-the-sand addict. "Communication is participation" he wrote, and he stressed the necessity of commitment. Obvious? Perhaps, but understressed and underapplied "at this time of world." David Showalter makes it plain that we have to hear ourselves before others can be expected to hear us. Before the book ends, he shows us how we can start achieving both elusive goals.

Warning in advance: Some of David Showalter's ideas are going to stay inside your head for keeps. They may even permanently damage your complacencies.

But start reading anyway. Enjoy the good talk and good sense, and don't fret about damages. If mental muscles become sore from unaccustomed exercise, be glad. Your head will be the better for it. Relax. Stay loose. Ride along. David Showalter doesn't offer you an easy, orderly journey from alpha to beta to gamma. His is a demanding, confusing safari from trial and error to success . . . maybe. In other words, life, life as it is, in the practical, human world. Take the trip, all of it, and one day, perhaps sooner than you expect, you'll get it done: You'll *say* it and they'll *hear* you.

Roy Meador
Ann Arbor, Michigan
January 14, 1973

List of Illustrations

Turn Left at Infinity? 12

Festina Lente or Hasten Slowly until You Catch Up
    with Where You're At 24

Which Bird Is Spinning? 36

The Sounder the Brass the Less the Polish 46

And Then at Last You will Succeed 56

Never Mind the Cold 68

The Many Splendored "Yep" 80

Waiting It Out with the C.O. or Second-Guesting
    a General 94

Is Anybody Happy? 112

Fatal but Possibly Not Painful 128

Daniel Boone: "I Was Never Lost, but Once I Was
    Confused for Three Days." 142

Table of Contents

A Beginning—Man and the Mechanism 1
   I Love that Wonderful Story 13
1 For Openers 15
   We Were Standing At 25
2 Non Legitimus Carborundum, or Words to that Effect 27
   Out of Apocrypha 37
3 Wha'd He Say? 39
   It Was a Grand 47
4 OK. So I'm Listening I'm Listening! To What? 49
   It Had Been a Long 57
5 Beginning Middle and End 59
   We Took a Bunch to Alaska 69
6 The Dynamics of Good, on Your Feet Presentation 71
   We Used to See Them 81
7 The Name of the Game 83
   The General Was Loaded 95
8 Smoke Signals 99
   We Had Been Aloft 113
9 Will Somebody Flip the Switch, Please? 117
   There He Was. In Person. 129
10 Promotion, Pay and Profit 133
   He Had Been Alone 143
Postscript 145

A Beginning—
Man and the Mechanism

I don't know the exact date—or even if it could be pinned down to that. Even in retrospect, the first symptoms of a serious malady are not easy to detect.

MAN

But I submit, for your consideration, that man in the 1960's re-discovered himself. A kind of frightening, dangerous, and sometimes fatal for some, experience, but rediscover himself he did. Or began to.

The Watts riot, a scary, almost unbelievable explosion of a group of people determined to break through the centuries-long intolerable dehumanization and degradation they had experienced, was a tragic part of this. So were the ensuing riots across the country along with the continuing upthrust of the newly identified "blacks." A kind of *chain reaction*, in a sense like a package of firecrackers exploding into a veritable arsenal of volatile munitions of practically every description and firepower, became a part of the everyday American scene for something like a decade. It promised to play for as long as the handbills lasted.

The incredible and horrifying assassinations of Kennedy and Martin Luther King; the murder of John F. Kennedy's assassin in plain sight of some 65 million televiewing homes; a nation of people stopped in their tracks for three days in a kind of compulsive witness of personal trauma, sorrow, loss and somehow individually shared responsibility, as their President was shot, attended to and finally laid to rest; the never-to-be-forgotten sight of chaos in the making in the hysterical panic attendant to another Kennedy glimpsed mortally wounded on the floor of a back service area at the Ambassador Hotel in Los Angeles, in an incredible replay of the naked brutishness of something gone mad in an otherwise earlier vintage rather quiet, lawabiding, respectable and peaceful society. All of it was direct and of that immediate moment, as it happened in front of our eyes with instant playback for those who missed the original.

The outbreak on college campuses across the country of demands, riots, sit-downs, sit-ins, demonstrations, bombings, marches, and probably inevitably, the shooting of students on two separate campuses.

Fish-ins to help the Indians. Chicano riots for Mexicans. Television appearances and appeals for understanding and acceptance of homosexuals. Programs for the disadvantaged, unintegrated, elderly, ill, socially maladjusted and psychologically deranged.

A whole *new* concept of life for the kids. Music of their own. Dress, hair and life style which, although strenuously rejected by their elders at first introductory blush, found a paralleling if more moderate simulation by that same rejecting group. Interestingly enough, both modes have striking resemblance to their forbears of the late 1800's.

An entire panoply of drugs, users, abuses and problems seemed to spring up overnight like a colony of monsters planted in ghostlike stealth in some secret, musty, fetid and multiplying cellar by a diabolical mastermind from outer space.

Hippies flourished. Communes were established. *Families* like the infamous Manson cult originated. Rock festivals rocked and echoed in a towering babel of sound, sex and sin. Courts were invaded and judges were threatened by unruly mobs. One was kidnaped at gunpoint and murdered.

Words like, *like* easily turned up like five times in a short sentence like attempted by those who like, for some reason or other, like found it like difficult to express themselves like otherwise. Other words equally over-used, such as *overview, interface, nitty-gritty, viable, body-count,* found their way into the vocabulary of a people looking for something which they were on the verge of discovering. Four letter words made the scene regardless of situation, circumstance, deference or courtesy. *Pornography flourished* and a rash of motion pictures flashed across the "silver screen" of America leaving nothing to the imagination. That four-letter Anglo-Saxon word, never before used in polite society, was as easy to find in conversation, a book, magazine, motion picture or play, as it once was found written on the walls of toilets. Its basic function was demonstrated in detail and color, in abandon, on film, in person, and at some of the public soul gatherings of the more lively among us.

And perhaps we should leave that side of it on that dreary note, with the rest of the illustrative material up to your own experience and imagination—something, incidentally, we once did with *class.*

The nation was in a shooting war which had never been formally declared. The gross national product was the highest it had ever been and so was the cost of living. A mild recession set in. The economy was called *overheated*, and was controlled to a certain extent by increasing interest rates. These in turn decreased when the economy became *undercooled*, and increased unemployment reared its ugly head.

It sometimes seemed that the only lift to the American spirit came from that sometimes heartstopping, always heartthrobbing drama in space. Certainly Neil Armstrong's foot visible on the ladder of the Yankee Clipper was the epitome of the timeless and mysterious spirit of mankind capable of prodigious feats. Man's first look via direct television at a towering, well nigh miraculous achievement first of its own, Man on the Moon, stirred us strongly not only at home but around the earth, plucking us bodily from the muck and mire that had us bogged to the armpits.

I am suggesting that someplace in all of this, man began to discover himself in a way that he had perhaps not had time for since the war to end wars ended on November 11th, 1918. For a few short years in that seemingly endless vista of peace, prosperity and picnics, with *progress* no great shucks or problem, man in the USA knew himself for what he was and made the most of it.

AND THE MECHANISM

Then came the milieu of the *mechanism*.

Henry Ford had something to do with it, as did Thomas Edison, Lee De Forest, Eli Whitney, Orville and Wilbur Wright, Alexander Graham Bell, and certainly Albert Einstein.

A BEGINNING 5

As that round wheel turned in all its uses, sizes and complexity; as those lights began flashing; as distance foreshortened, disappeared, was overcome or became luxurious, comfortable and bearable; the population exploded and was conditioned, educated and trained to meet the need, which any way you philosophize, rationalize or intellectualize about it spells p-r-o-f-i-t. The mechanism to achieve this single, singular and monolithic goal was developed in all its many faceted splendor, capability and truly magnificent expertise.

It had some attendant problems however. It had its recompense and reward in, higher wages, improved working conditions, shorter hours, more leisure time than man had ever thought possible, peripheral benefits, retirement, an infinity of material means, social and medical security, ease and comfort. It all came, however, and I think we need to bear it in mind, because of and after the fact of, *profit*.

From simple survival through the intermediate ranges and on up to that high plateau of individual outreach called self-realization, profit underwrote it, profit made it possible, and profit maintained it.

But, as they say, *it began to lose something in the translation.* In the midst of all that plenty, practically buried under an infinitely munificent shower of baubles, bangles and beads, giftwrapped, perfumed, advertised and promoted for the better things in life, man hit a kind of troublesome hang-up. He had never had it so good since Eve first took that bite out of the apple in the Garden of Eden. But *his pesky rib* came to bother him once in a while.

A house with a bath and three quarters. Daylight basement, game room with pool table. Swimming pool. Three bedrooms and a master bedroom with walk-in closet and exclusive bathroom. The rest of the house, appliances and appurtenances to match. Two cars, a camper and a boat. Property and a cabin on a lake. Golf clubs, skis, guns, power tools, cameras, projectors and screen, appliances, conveniences, equipment of all description.

Money in the bank, savings account, stocks and bonds, annuities, credit cards, insurance for emergencies, contingencies, possibilities and probabilities, memberships in associations, organizations and clubs, social status and wardrobe to match.

Trips to Rome, Greece and New Zealand. Vacations in Hawaii, the Caribbean, the Mediterranean and Canada. Weekends in Reno, Las Vegas, Los Angeles, Mexico City. Business jaunts to New York, Chicago, Washington D.C., Dallas, San Francisco, Seattle, Tokyo, Berlin, London, Paris, Copenhagen, Moscow. Conferences in Sydney, Shanghai and Tel Aviv.

Even though—jetting from East to West—you could eat breakfast three times from England to the West Coast of the United States of America and still get it all down before noon, you still couldn't quite catch up with yourself. As ridiculous as that might seem, even as a remotely possible annoyance with all that gilt edge at your fingertips, it gave man pause to consider when he could find time for it.

Then there was that *snapper* for the universe provided by Professor Einstein, which of itself was an attitude-changer for the world, its competitors and neighbors and private citizens. Its already demonstrated destructive power and thermo-nuclear threat, capable of returning man to the Stone Age, was omnipresent.

The immediate, direct, on-the-spot, right where it was happening impact of the most dynamic, instantaneous and far-reaching news medium ever developed, really gave man something to consider, at ease, relaxed, comfortable and receptive in his own living room.

In all that compress of progress; catch-up after World War II; press and pressure of competitive business; moves toward giant octopian corporate structure; Korea and Vietnam, and the to-the-brink gamesmanship of the great powers with no place for the leader but out in front; in the race for space, including that new associate—discovered, jawed over and beaten to a pulp—ecology; the unceasing stridency of abrasive strife and violence in all matters affecting our welfare and well-being, *man was caught between a rock and a hard place.*

Two other ingredients were contributors to the concoction of this giant stew, which, after sufficient ingestion, was to bring us to our feet in all strata of society, retching and vomiting in indignation and rebellion.

One was the planned programming and control of our lives from first breath to last gasp, by the *quote* experts *unquote* and the *quote* expertise *unquote* employed therein, thereinunder, thereto and from that date everforward, Amen! There is nothing wrong with *expert* or *expertise* as such. It is simply its inhuman application, implied, practiced and mountainously overdone, that contains in it the veritable seeds of disaster and catastrophe. Witness the year of our Lord, 1971, and its approximate preceding decade. No *expert*, be he politician, bureaucrat, educator, religionist, philosopher, civil servant, businessman, citizen or whatever, will even begin to recognize what we are discussing here, because nobody, in the first place tells an *expert* what to do. That's what he tells you. In the second, and even more frightening, place he is out to save you and the world—his way. So was Hitler. So was Stalin. So is any self-seeking power centrist in the world—from husbands to bosses to absolute monarchs of whatever they survey, under whatever guise.

Mark that one up someplace *buddy boy,* and never lose sight of it.

The other ingredient, symbolizing and further activating this de-personalization that the *mechanism* has been foisting off on us for too many years, is called computerization. One of the most significant defects, to me, in this marvellous machine, occurred during the Apollo XIV flight. With man ready to set down on the moon, willing, able, endlessly trained for the task, (and for my money of absolutely heroic stature), the computer programmed it for "abort." Should this have been carried through, with no way found to circumvent the computer, its result could have wiped out the program. In effect it could have: cancelled the billions of dollars invested in it; lost us our position of adventure and achievement in space; further contributed to unemployment; discouraged those pioneering scientists, specialists and technicians in that field; or shot a hole in or bolstered our economy, (depending on how you look at it).

I'm not, for a moment, arguing yes or no in space, right or wrong, should we or shouldn't we. I am simply stating a practical and observable fact that relates directly to the subject at hand.

Man was created to control his own destiny, his own individual destiny, as badly as he might muddle it or as proficiently as he might succeed. The expert may advise and suggest within those limiting bounds which keep him on the same human plane as the rest of us, but play God he may not. The machine can assist and help. But neither can violate that miraculous indestructibility that is the individual.

REDISCOVERY

I propose to this audience that, someplace along the line in these last years, somehow this remarkable, humble, proud, unpredictable, far more intelligent than he is generally given credit for, individual, began to get *the message.*

Further, all the resultant strife, near-chaos, rebellion, segmented-group-anarchy, in which he finds himself, like it or not, is, pure and simple, *man's rediscovery of himself*—as an individual.

From his experience in life as a *husband, father, producer, worker, war veteran, home owner, tax payer and voting citizen,* he tucked some useful and valuable experience and knowledge between his ears and behind his furrowed brow.

As today's child growing up exposed to instant information of any and all description as near as the switch on a TV set, he is far more knowledgeable, more widely informed on a diversity of subjects than his parents, and much more inclined to question the world and its circumstances than his parents or grandparents in their time.

As a member of any racial, ethnic, or any kind of an apartheid status group—whether by birth, circumstance or preference—what he did not or does not have, denied altogether, what he has no part of, participation or sharing in, is not only obvious through various communicating means, but painfully so because of his rather lately acquired awareness. Automobiles, schools, television, radio, newspapers, movies, all helped put this together for him.

None of us, with all this background of experience, however you choose to delineate it, could then sit in the middle of the damnedest communicating din, clatter and cacophony and not be aware of ourselves as individual human beings, as a collective brotherhood—no matter how disparate—of human beings, and that our conduct with each other, if not *downright murderous,* assassinating, felonious, dishonest, segregating, massing, rapacious, at least left something to be desired.

We were horrified, shocked, amazed, angry, rebellious and in downright despair, at what we saw of ourselves.

Some so much so, caught in the mechanistic maw that so patently overlooked and ignored the basic human values, that they took the do-or-die course to secure that individuality. Hence the beginning of man's rediscovery of himself and the opening of all gaps by whatever name called, by whatever group initiated, by whatever nomenclature and dialectic employed. Some of them just as immoral, inimical and sub-human as they can be.

All of us, who rebelling in one degree or another within the confines of constitutional legitimacy and human decency, regardless of whether we like the association or not, have *one thing in common*. The violation of the human being by some kind of mechanism, in a fashion that is dehumanizing and degrading. *We have another thing in common*. The ability to shunt that incursion aside by putting our capability to control it to work.

And we have one more thing in common. The means by which we accomplish that objective. *Communication*. At that point in the corridor of re-entry I would like to meet you at the door, hold it open for you, and hope that we learn something terribly important and useful to us—together.

What we learn together is going to depend in large part on opening our minds as well as the door. How well we get along in the *terra incognita*, the unknown wilderness country of Communication will be determined by the wide-eyed courage we take along as luggage. And the willingness, not just the ability, the *willingness* to see when the big truth of a misused word is slowly eaten away by little jackal lies. Nerve is needed, and memorized maps, and strangers to give directions. Just as important as nerve and maps and strangers will be a hearty knapsack filled with determination. It takes determination to get anywhere in the country of Communication, to hustle the truth from its flabby sheath of contradictions, to keep going and get there even when "you can't get there."

"What do we mean by 'getting there'?" Simple. We mean talking to one another, putting it over, getting the message across, breaking through the oatmeal of confusion, tune-out, and fear. We mean *Communicating.*

Turn Left At Infinity?

VIGNETTE

I LOVE THAT WONDERFUL STORY about the traveler in a strange country—however you prefer to characterize it as long as you keep it in the U. S., and defined as a first time visitor to our Southland.

He has reached a point of decision, or indecision, and has stopped along the roadside to inquire his way of a native.

"How do you get to Clements from here?" he asks.

Feller sizes him up, shoves his hat back on his head, looks one way and t'other, squints his eyes, shifts his tobacco plug, expectorates.

"You go down the road a piece here," he says, "until you come to a fork in it. Big oak tree in the middle. Turn left there for about five miles, an' then ———"

"Nope," he says. "Whyn't you turn yourself right around, and head back until you come to a big old two story farmhouse, sittin' up on top of a hill 'bout a minutes dog trot off the road. At the next cross road turn right and drive on until you come to ———"

"Lessee. If you'll just take that next turnin' you seep up the road there. Then if you'll follow that. A purty, windin' road it is up over Hawg Mountain an' down the other side to Pincher Creek. May have a little trouble fordin' it this time of year. Once acrosst, the road sort of meanders off to the left until you come to Three Forks. You got a choice there a little confusin' to some folks, but no mind. Just bear off to the north which should put you into Ribcage Flats by ———"

"Well," he considers, "Guess that wont get you there either. Best go down to Millersville, an' the first turnin' to your left, a mite over two miles from town, you take the old switchback, nowheres near as difficult as some might think ——"

"Come to think of it," he says, "You can't get there from here."

It's a dandy story, worth the compliment of a healthy chortle. We can laugh and go our way because we know it isn't true. What the protector of Hawg Mountain really means is that he's never gotten there from here. Thank him, traveler, and keep searching.

1

For Openers

"Jump!", the man says.

"How high?"

"Now?"

"Who do you think you are?"

"Drop dead!"

"Which way?"

"I'm afraid of height!"

"With my eyes open?"

"You gotta be kidding!"

"Not unless Jones jumps first!"

A few responses, not abnormal or unnatural, to what would seem to be a very simple effort at communication, should you step into the middle of a group and issue that command badly.

Jump, at first blush, is an uncomplicated four letter word. It needs no handy dictionary to tell you what it means. The word spoken in English, or its equivalent—to those of other language persuasions—is probably plainly understood by all from age four onward. It means—*jump*! Get yourself off the solid on which you are presently located, into space, by whatever physical expenditure of effort necessary on your part. Frequently it takes the form of some sort of command that has an urgent nature to it.

If you're in rattlesnake country; know about rattlers and their nasty habits, when somebody yells "Jump!" you jump and start running even before you hit the ground, and with no equivocation whatsoever.

When the "Jumpmaster" says *"Jump!"* there might be a fair possibility you can't remember or accurately pronounce, "Geronimo!"—but about the command there is no doubt. Nor is there any doubt about what you are supposed to do. Post haste. Not to mention forthwith.

Should that crusty old curmudgeon, known as *boss*, by whatever the title, issue that simple four letter exclamatory command, even though it may have no faintly discernible intelligent relationship to the task at hand, you get the message.

Were you, however, to walk into the midst of one hundred people, unknown to you and you to them, knowing that their lives depended on jumping instantaneously as you shouted the command without any chance to explain it to them, it is extremely doubtful that anybody would *jump*. Your chances would improve somewhat if you had a few minutes to introduce yourself, your mission, and why those one hundred unknowns should jump. Their chances would improve considerably given a similar set of circumstances with people known intimately to you and

FOR OPENERS   17

you to them. But, in both situations you would still have some who never got off the ground.

The word, *jump*, is simple enough. The circumstance, particularly the human element, is not. How well delineated and understood those circumstances need to be is the subject of our discussion.

COMMUNICATION DEFINED

Communication means, "Using whatever signal you have at hand, in order to relate specifically to whomever you are addressing yourself in such fashion as to secure some kind of definitive action. Preferably in your favor."

More simply, *getting somebody to do something for you.*

From that launch pad the communication missile can manage to abort, make an appointment in Samara, ride with the Four Horsemen of the Apocalypse, or go into orbit—even though that was not at all your intention.

Communication is, in truth, our *lifeline*. Without it we couldn't make love, money or progress. It is both the simple and complex means by which we survive. It is, in fact, the single, most important fact or facet of life. Without it, life as we know it, would not exist.

It is amazing therefore how well we do manage to get along communicating as ineptly and inexpertly as we do. Or, it is no surprise at all that we get along as badly as we do because we are execrable communicators as a race of people, as a nation, and as individuals.

Ask your wife, kids, secretary, employees, friends, and the guy to whom you just tried to explain what you wanted done to the car. Ask the kids today—if you can find a credible means of getting to them (and I submit you can)—who not only have lost contact with us, but faith as well.

Sit across the luncheon table one-to-one with a very angry black, an implacable enemy, thoroughly and utterly convinced that Whitey isn't really hearing anything the blacks are saying. No more that is, than necessary to keep the boat from being rocked.

Hear the clang and clangor on college campuses, the clamorous outcry of all minority groups, (sometimes even the majorities)—the young, the black, the poor, the old, the disadvantaged, the flower people, the addicts, the criminals, Women's Lib and even the Gay Society.

But let's not go so far afield, or into such controversial areas, that the subject matter of this presentation sinks precipitately without a trace in the Western sunset.

When we talk about the *generation* or *credibility* gap we are talking about communication and its lack of effective application, for whatever the reasons or lack thereof—depending on which way you hear the problem.

COMMUNICATOR, SUBJECT, AUDIENCE

Communicating involves three basic factors. Communicator. Subject. Audience. Its principal problem, hangup and challenge is that obtusely imprecise, unpredictable, emotional, sometimes wonderful sometimes awful, yet unquestionably miraculous being, genus homo sapiens—God bless his beating heart, independent mind and unconquerable spirit—who is today in deadly peril and fear of losing his identity.

FOR OPENERS   19

It is no wonder that most of us have a liking—shy away from as a matter of fact—for any kind of formal communicating process, any kind of personal presentation on one's feet in front of a group. While we may not individually be able to scientifically, psychologically or by whatever logical and scholary measurement we can apply, specify why we don't like or want to address any convocation of our fellows on any subject at any time at any place, instinctively we recognize a stacked deck when we see one.

If however, communication is as important as we have been told it is by heads of state, business, industry, labor, management, the establishment, majorities, minorities, conformists, nonconformists, religion, the sacred estate of marriage and its several offshoots, and that quietly suffering, lonely individual who needs to be heard almost above everything else, it would be interesting to see just how much any one of us, individually, is willing to put of himself into that communicating process in order to make it work better than it does. For you. For me. For society and whatever of its aspects which may have particular meaning for us.

The next problem in communicating, a blood relation of its primary roadblock (you and me) is simply one of slothfulness. It takes plain hard work to communicate, or even begin to communicate effectively.

Finally, there is no great big dark secret to the tools of the communicating art. They can be and are very simple or very complex or any combination thereof. They run the gamut from a single facial expression to the doggonedest crackup of audio/visual aids you ever did see!

If there is any secret at all to the business of communicating, one to one, one to several, several to several, or even on it to

HOW TO SAY IT SO THEY HEAR IT

those frightening astronomics, one to several million television homes, it is this: You may not win a single vote, an inch of ground, an improvement in your profit and loss statement, or a pat on the back, man being the wonderfully indeterminate, independent soul he is.

Next, from that candidly practical ground zero, don't ever forget that it *is* man, the human quotient with whom and which you are dealing, and that your only hope of securing the action in your favor voluntarily, willingly and in real cooperation, is to proceed exclusively on that premise.

Then it would be helpful if you were acquainted with the *tools of the communicating art* and how to use them.

Finally I would like to suggest you *do your homework*. Diligently. Thoroughly. Painstakingly.

We will explore the areas of talesmanship, technique and tools of the communicating process together in the next few pages. Not as a hard and fast handbook, but as a probing, participating guideline which you yourself will have some part in developing and in the end result will either put it to work or not in your own attempt to improve your communicating ability, in your own inimitable style.

That we need to improve there is no question. That we want to improve is in doubt. That we can improve is a certainty—provided we are willing to invest and risk something of ourselves in learning how to communicate better.

If there is an urgent need for any kind of specialized capability today, that is not only current but renewably so, it is certainly in the field of communicating. Not as we have known it or consider it to be at this point, for we haven't really examined more than its surface, but with more emphasis in terms of the basic recognition of the human factor, quotient, need and identity.

FOR OPENERS 21

I would like to suggest early in this discourse that there is not only a specialized field here in what we are to examine together, but *a rather remarkable opportunity* for the management which decides to put it to work for whatever it is that management is managing, and for the individual who decides to help management put this to work, as say, the director of communication.

(Decision makers please note.)

This is not to say or infer that communication as we will specify it interferes with or impinges upon advertising or public relations. Both professions have separate functions of their own, and although communication is their goal, as indeed it is with the news media, neither advertising or public relations has seen fit, found time or found it necessary to include this specialized communicating function within their aegis. It is difficult enough I am sure to manage those particular specialties.

Perhaps we need a new name for it. If so somebody will certainly come up with it, but I have yet to find a company president or administrative decision maker, who, complaining about the problem of communication as a prime concern has turned to his advertising or public relations department or agency, for an answer.

In the first place when the *boss* complains about communication he is usually talking about inter-company, inter-department, boss to department head to employee, employee to customer, person to person, people to people relationships. Interpersonal communication. He is not talking about a press release or feature or interview, commercial, four color advertisement or billboard. That's a complaint of its own and in a special register to accompany it.

There is even the possibility of another culprit—the communicating blackout he experienced with his wife that very morning and its resultant red-edged fogged eyesight almost involving him in a serious automobile accident on his way to the office. His communicating syndrome, apparently inadequate earlier with his wife had improved at this juncture to the point where it was simple, explicit, colorful and punctuated by a loud and prolonged blast on the horn as he addressed his fellow motorist. The return, equally direct, to the point and impossible to misunderstand or misinterpret simply meant—*"The same to you, buddy!"*

Our technology in the general field of communication is superb. Sometimes, at best however, it seems to have outrun our individual, collective and corporate ability to understand, use or even cope with it. While some of this certainly must be charged to misuse, even stupidity in some flagrant cases—perhaps better defined as failure to accurately assess and respond to the gut level we have been discussing—perhaps the biggest problem of all is that we haven't defined what we mean when we say communication. *What* is it? *What* is its function? *How* do we put it to work for us with people directing the effort who understand it and are capable of managing it effectively?

I suspect that is the real problem. My objective and hope is, that in discussing this together we can come up with an approach and a practical beginning that specifies the ground rules for a game that threatens to get away from us.

Too much is lost if we merely shrug and let it go. In communications "the game that got away" would be most of the things, stuff, and notions that we nervously but stubbornly call our civilization. If the game is moving too fast for us, like a comet chewing its own tail, I think there are available ways to catch up, or if need be, to slow the game down. And why not. *"We're"* the bosses. We can fly or drive or, time permitting and the weather nice, walk. Communication, "like" Thurber's knight, may have a tendency to dash madly off in all directions. A bit of effort together, and we can change *madly* to *effectively*.

Festina Lente or Hasten Slowly until you catch up with where you're at.

VIGNETTE

WE WERE STANDING AT, or around the bar at the Variety Club in Hollywood.

They were gathered around and listening to Jimmie Mattern, pioneer aviator and holder of many world records in aviation's early history. There were some directors and writers, some greater and lesser lights sprinkled with the salt and pepper of other entertainment industry types.

Jimmie was holding forth on his first-time experience as a guest in the left seat of a four-engine jet. His background for those who don't remember or know him—barnstorming, seat-of-the-pants, hell-for-leather, shove the throttle to the firewall and pray for an opening in the murk, flying.

A natural born story teller, he had been developing the then rather newborn air and jet age, how miraculous it is, its accomplishments and achievement, and its fanfaring future.

We were all zeroed in on Jimmie, so intent on what he was saying, you could hardly hear the clink of ice against a glass.

"Just think of it," he said, "We used up more fuel in that big 707 taxiing to the end of the runway than I used in my 'round-the-world flight." We pondered that one for a silent moment.

"My gosh," he said, "You can fly from here to New York in 4½ hours."

There was another pause. Then cutting through the silence in a soft, almost inaudible underplay, came the voice of Wallace Ford.

"I don't know," he said. "I'd rather take the train. Who needs me in 4½ hours?"

It takes all kinds to make a Twentieth Century. And we're still getting there, whether by jet, or train, or a bicycle built for two. The hurry-uppers have their place. Likewise the slow-downers. What we have to watch out for are the grind-to-a-halters, the ones who insist on not being heard, who can't get there because they're disinclined to choose a place to get. Helping them choose is also part of the game.

2

Non Legitimus Carborundum, Or Words To That Effect

Let's look as best we can, without aid or succor from professional anthropology, sociology or psychology, at the guy in the eye of a hurricane towards whom all this communicating gobbledegook is directed.

First of all let's assume, as a basic thesis, that the individual *is* the object of any communicating effort, and that it *is* important that he be kept in sight and on target at all times. As at least one didactic pragmatism in this presentation this one is the most awesomely requiring of all. If we are to have an earthly chance of getting *people* to hear what we say, it is totally dependent upon recognizing them as *people*, treating them as *people*, and communicating with them as *people*.

If that seems so ridiculously obvious as to be cause for you to close the book at this point considering the whole thing a waste of time—don't give up. *There's more.*

How many times lately, for example, in conversation with someone; listening to anyone from a president of a company to a foreman to a friend; on the receiving end of a speech; viewing or listening to a commercial; reading or listening to the news or editorial comment, or as a participant in a meeting, seminar or convention, have you felt—inferior, stupid, uninformed, misinformed, useless, hurt, embarrassed, used, taken advantage of, irritated, outraged, alienated or downright furiously angry? Not necessarily because of any inadequacy on your part, but because the communicator made you feel that way by what he did, by what he said, by his attitude, by what he didn't say or didn't do?

AUDIENCE TURN-OFF

Sure it isn't all like that. But a surprising amount of communicating is, for a surprising number of people, for a surprising number of ordinary people-reasons.

How come? What happened? First off probably something like this.

Generally you responded in the exact manner in which you were approached. Action gets a like reaction unless you happen to be something other than human yourself, or have developed a remarkable degree of restraint.

Let's take the reactions listed above and imagine some fairly typical circumstances which might have caused any one of us to receive end trauma.

INFERIOR Your immediate supervisor, to whom you are directly responsible—he knows it and never lets you forget it—

never misses an opportunity to let you know, preferably in front of somebody else, that he considers you inefficient, inadequate, incapable and just barely able to hang on to your job. If he had his way about it and could manipulate it, you would be fired immediately.

STUPID Someone you like, respect or love, and from whom you want the same in return, lectures you, bawls you out, criticizes you—usually under the guise of constructive criticism—in an area or on a subject where you have goofed, made some kind of error or mistake, the kind of mistake that anybody could make and certainly not the mountain that your molehill got.

UNINFORMED "You haven't paid much attention to what's going on lately, have you?" "Don't you ever listen to the news?" "I thought everybody knew better than that!" "Man, every trailer owner with a lick of sense knows you shouldn't do that!" "You should have known better!" And on, and on. Sometimes by inference or lack of comment, as well as by spoken word.

MISINFORMED An expert, (that's what the folder said), in a formal presentation before a group misrepresents the facts as you know them to be. A commentator bases his expert evaluation on an obvious personal hangup or prejudice. An officer of a company refuses to level with you on a point on which there is no valid reason why he shouldn't do anything other than level with you.

USELESS A fellow employee, foreman or supervisor, takes over a facet of your job, which may be new to you or have developed during an emergency or crisis, leaving you with nothing to do as well as with the feeling he doesn't think you could do it anyhow.

HURT Your boss made you feel like a dummy for not doing something the way he wanted it done. It was a lousy idea in the first place. He explained it very poorly and didn't give you a chance to get it clarified.

EMBARRASSED The speaker addressing your group is not only poorly prepared, but apologetic for it.

USED—TAKEN ADVANTAGE OF You have sold a difficult bill of goods—for your company, an organization, a belief, a project, your boss, a friend—which is found to be completely invalid because of misrepresentation, dishonesty or for some basic lack of integrity.

IRRITATED The speaker addressing your group has not gone to the trouble of inquiring about or assessing its moral temperature. The dirty story he tells is out of place (more on that later), in effect cancelling his effectiveness as a communicator and thereby wasting your time as a listener.

OUTRAGED The guest on a television program deliberately misinterprets a question directed towards him in a very delicate situation with explosive potential. His calculated polemic and prejudiced answer to what was intended as a fair question with a possibility of a fair answer sets off the divisive time bomb and more fuel is added to the already burning fire.

ALIENATED Any one of the above communicating errors, intentional or unintentional, can become cause for dissatisfaction, partial or total alienation, and can negate any communicating effort we are making.

DOWNRIGHT, FURIOUSLY ANGRY Let's say, for our purpose, that man is the result of his total experience. Add into that, if you like, heritage, education, background and infinitum. Lots of infinitum. Without much or any conscious effort at all, he remembers those keys on that "88" of his that are dissonant, off-register, cacophonous, clangy, ear-splitting, headache producing, stomach upsetting, and downright destroying. When somebody or some tune hits one of those sensitive keys he reacts just as any human being does who has just been kicked in the slats instead of being treated like a human. A fellow human being. Lack of communication can frequently be translated as, "man's inhumanity to man."

Now before we take too roseate a view as we glance blandly over our critique of that communicator who just got his foot in his mouth, remember that you and I are going to grab for the same brass ring. All that we have said here applies equally to us anytime we step onto that same brilliant-hued, exhilarating, dizzying and sometimes dangerous steam calliopeed *merry-go-round*.

SLOW DOWN!

Okeh. Let's recap a little.

The *individual* is the object of any and all communication.

The human being individual. He is not rich, poor, disadvantaged, old or young. He is neither white, black, brown or yellow. He is not boss, employee, big shot, hard hat, hawk, dove, republican, democrat, socialist, communist, establishment, rebel, smart, stupid, intellectual, bigot, liberal or conservative.

HUMANS, NOT LABELS

Sure. He is all those things, a part and parcel of them. As a communicator you certainly need to recognize and consider the *label*.

If you are going to get through to him however, if you are really going to get through to him, you must not treat him as a *label*. He must not be treated as a *label*. He must be considered, treated and communicated with first, last and always, as an individual.

By all means there are exceptions. If you want a favorable response from an audience already partial to your viewpoint, stance or attitude, go ahead and label away. If you want. I still wouldn't recommend it. As a suggestion, I believe it to be one of the biggest mistakes we make in communication today. Even the most strictured group is composed of individuals who are capable of cerebrating, analyzing and making decisions. If you elect to go the *labelling* route, and with some segments you don' treally have much alternative choice, it better have in it as well, something of factual fair play along with its partisanship. In our game of majorities today's winner is tomorrow's loser. We meet the same people coming back down as we met going up, and they have long and accurate memories.

The object of our communicating effort is the individual, regardless of what he may have labelled himself. He has an imprint, heritage, experience, education, intelligence, personality, outlook, integrity and spirit all his own. His *unique*, unto him, fingerprints unduplicated in all humanity symbolize, if we think about it, his equally unique individuality.

Think about that one for a little when you think about communicating. Or before you attempt it.

It is obscene to expect therefore that we can communicate with him on anything other than the individual, human being level. That's how we expect to be communicated with isn't it? Consider your audience then as human beings, not labels.

Don't think, incidentally, we're talking about an *absolute* that has no flexibility, fallibility, exception, or room for failure. Anyone of us who can totally accomplish what I am suggesting here can probably walk on water too. It does not, however, remove it from being the prime requisite position, nor does it excuse us from setting the individual as our communicating goal.

NON LEGITIMUS CARBORUNDUM

Lest somebody misunderstand we are not talking either about revolutionizing the world, changing society or any segment of it. We are talking about *communicating* and the principal thesis around which and upon which it can successfully cornerstone. We are also talking about the every workaday world, the plain hard work of the communicator.

For some reason this reminds me of what had been for me a very successful evening of communication some years ago. A tremendous turnout of people for what previously had been a rather dull annual event. Public service (free) time on network radio with a program literally star studded with personalities from the motion picture, radio and entertainment business. Principal speaker one of the most famous motion picture stars of all time—Robert Young. All had been my responsibility to dream up, develop, promote, publicize and ride herd on.

After the event, I, by happenstance, ran into the President of our organization, who, at best, was a rather remote individual removed from the common herd. I made the mistake, in my overflowing exuberance of asking him what he thought of the program.

"Fine," he replied. *"What have you got planned for tomorrow?"*

As an idea of what I have been talking about here, in the length of time passed, the violation it represents of the overrun of the individual, and the fact that I still remember it, I pass it along to you for whatever it is worth.

NEXT?

The individuals with whom you communicate will react.

How they react is something else. Exactly what some communicators have been heard to mutter under their breath after a confrontation with an audience, "Man, that was really something else!"

There are some probabilities, some possibilities, some impossibilities, and *would you believe* some surprises.

Some of them pleasant.

And perhaps trick number one will be mastering the techniques of communication, both *sending* and *receiving*, while remaining our own cranky, cantankerous, lovable selves. Baron Von Richthofen is Baron Von Richthofen and a sparrow is a sparrow. And a rose is a rose. Anyway they used to be.

Which Bird Is Spinning?

VIGNETTE

OUT OF THE APOCRYPHA of that intrepid race of men, the forbears of men in space, those who flew with the leather helmet, goggles, silk neck scarf, britches and puttees, comes some first class Americana.

One of that gentry, as the story goes, flying in an open cockpit Jennie, Swallow or Waco—or some such vintage— noticed an eagle flying chase on him.

"More than that," he relates, "When I banked, he banked. When I dipped, he dipped. When I climbed, he climbed. So naturally I began to check him out."

"I banked, turned, dipped, figure-eighted, looped. No matter what I did, the eagle was right with me."

"Okeh, old baldie," I said to myself, "Try this one on for size. Whereupon," he continued, "I yanked it up and into a stall, let her fall off into a spin. Then I looked around. Sure enough old brother eagle was right in there spinnin' with the best of 'em."

"I let her go until I didn't have much room left to put out, kicked it out of the spin, and levelled off."

"How about the eagle?" Somebody interposed in the dramatic pause.

"Donno," the barnstormer replied, "Last time I looked, he was still spinnin'."

It is difficult, this business of perspective in a crowded universe, last time we looked. Among the intrepid race of eagles, they tell about the big, ugly, crazy bird that sedulously aped an eagle and was last seen heading down down down in a foolishly persistent spin. Men and eagles talk to themselves but not to one another. Could that be the problem? One of them?

3

Wha'd He Say?

LISTENING

The other and equally important part of who really heard you lately is its reverse—*who have you really listened to lately?*

Listening is an absolute essential and requirement of good communication. As a matter of fact a major part of it begins there.

The next time you are a part of any conversational group, sit back and relax. Nobody is going to miss you anyhow in this kind of conversational fiasco. *Listen and observe.* Play a game with yourself—use the Richter earthquake scale if you like. Rate the conversationalists on their ability to communicate, on how what they have said and are saying was really listened to by the group, or even by any member of the group. Remember, seven on the Richter scale is a real devastator. If you find anybody who gets beyond two, congratulations!

You will be aware of, I am sure, and will probably indeed have fallen into the same trap, the, "I can't wait until he finishes so I can plunge in," syndrome. You get the feeling that nobody is interested at all in what anybody is saying except as a leadoff for the next participant. Transitions from subject to subject can be, and are, totally irrelevant.

Maybe the purpose of such conversation has no relation whatsoever with the kind of communicating we're talking about. Maybe that's not its point at all. But it certainly indicates one solid fact—the need to communicate we all feel. Perhaps it serves its purpose that way in a kind of frantic, frenetic fellowship that makes the participants feel part of a group, or on the other hand forces participation to keep from feeling excluded.

One way or another it is an excellent example of the kind of *non-listenership* so many of us find ourselves guilty of.

It doesn't have to be a conversational group of people. Observe two individuals, who can find, for whatever the reason, no means, no way or even possibility of, communication. To state it as simply as possible, aware of the immediate question from all kinds of demurrers from the professional wings, they can't communicate because they don't want to. For a whole packet of reasons they don't want to.

The attempt at communication in this specific can be so emotional, frustrating and completely upsetting, that the two individuals involved would rather not make the effort at all. It will go no place and they know it. Neither individual hears the other at all, and neither can possibly speak or communicate in any fashion that will be heard, understood or accepted by the other—outside of blows that is.

Bring it to the job level. Can you think of anyone with whom you do business, or in your company, whom you can't talk to because he doesn't listen?

Two-way communication—*sending and receiving*—is absolutely essential if the circuit is to effectively complete. One-way communication—*sending and no receiving*—is no communication. Oh we hear to a degree, partially, inaccurately, uninterestedly, uncooperatively and the job that was to be done is performed in just about the same degree.

THE SENDER

Let's look at listening from the very practical viewpoint of the *sender*.

Why is it important to listen at all? Any good actor can answer that one. You get your cues from listening. Cues and clues to all sorts of interesting things for the sender. First of all let's look at some of the reasons for not hearing what someone is saying, or, at best, finding it extremely difficult to hear what he is saying.

Not being treated as an individual is a prime roadblock, in the same category as the sender who talks down to you. It's probably one of the quickest roads to communicating oblivion, yet how frequently we find it employed. How we stumble over this one is difficult to explain since it is instantaneously recognized by tots who don't know the word for it to tottering ancients who have had a lifetime full of it. It's as phony as *a three-dollar bill* and just as identifiable. By osmosis, by extra-sensory perception, by native acuity, by whatever process, we know when we are being talked down to. We tune the sender out immediately, and turn him off altogether if he persists.

Talking down to cuts the sender off from the receiver as quickly as the flip of a light switch for the very basic reason that the listener is aware of this instantaneously and resents it automatically. The listener has simply been placed in a position of inferiority. He knows it, isn't about to accept it, nor should he. He may be in a lesser or different position, by reason of job, social status, income, wealth, but not on a fellow human basis. Not by a long shot!

Danny Kaye and Bill Cosby flash into mind immediately as illustrative of the principle involved. Adults as a class of people are not particularly noted for their ability to communicate effectivey with youngsters—and *vice versa*. But Kaye and Cosby represent perfection itself in communication with kids. They talk to them, entertain them, have fun with them on the same level. *Genuinely.*

Any time we, as communicators, are not on straight and level flight with our audience, we're out of touch, out of communication, and out of business. Any condescension on our part, any false position, any assumption of superiority other than that accorded us by the audience, is as obvious as egg on our face. When that happens we may as well be home listening to ourself on the tape recorder.

We don't hear very well either if the sender or message is counterfeit, phony or dishonest. These traits are not always easy to discern. Witness the bunco squads who annually deal with our inability to tell the good guys from the bad guys without a program. However in terms of a communicator on his feet and on view for a period of time such deceiving traits become more readily observable. A gesture, a word, a nervous movement, something begins to give it away, and the audience goes away with it. Abraham Lincoln said it, *"You can fool some of the people some of the time; you can fool some of the people all of the time, but you can't fool all of the people all of the time."* Not too shabby as a communicating precept!

Television has its critics, but in today's instant, on and in full view, wide world, presentation of people, we have a remarkable opportunity to assess those who would lead, guide and direct us in all of its varying gradient. It is no wonder that the medium scares them to death, from amateurs to professionals. It is such an unforgiving instrument. The slightest character anomaly, momentarily ambivalent attitude, on your feet incapability or inadequacy, is glaringly delineated.

Along with that, however, some very useful indices are on view and in plain sight, with an immediacy, exposure and exposition of the individual involved, absolutely unheard of and nonexistent prior to TV. It was improved by ear and immediacy with the advent of radio, but it still missed that all important *sight* factor.

The fact is that the majority of people—majorities that is on both sides of any issue, for and against—are not as easiy duped as some would have us believe. What I am suggesting here is, that whether you as a communicator are pro or con, facts are heard in your favor. Counterfeit is not only not heard in your favor, it can kill you without chance or prayer for a redeeming and repeat performance.

WHY WE DON'T LISTEN

We don't hear—don't really listen to—others for a lot of simple reasons. We don't hear somebody who bullies us, threatens us, bosses us around. We don't hear someone who is patently unfair, unkind, discourteous, critical or complaining. We find it totally impossible to hear somebody who disapproves of us—about on the same level of hearing rejection as those who are constantly teaching us a lesson, never missing the opportunity to moralize.

We don't hear anyone who is rude, boorish, opinionated, prejudiced or bigoted. We don't like to be *tolerated*—part of talking down to and not being treated like an individual human being with valid values of our own.

We tend to stop listening to the person who does not listen to us, who short circuits the communicating process. We don't hear the individual who hurts our feelings, embarrasses us, uses or takes advantage of us.

In short perhaps the best way to express it is to say, simply, *we don't hear anybody who doesn't hear us.*

Yet it is absolutely essential that we hear and listen to other people if we are going to communicate at all, and, as a matter of fact sometimes indeed if we are going to survive.

You can spell *survive* a variety of ways. As a husband or wife. As an employee or employer. As a free people or faceless recruits in Big Brother's automated chain gang. Some can't hear ever because they have mastered too thoroughly the megalomaniacal art of listening only to themselves. Though they own the earth and crack whips with chimes, they don't really survive. Not forever. Not long.

The sounder the brass the less the polish.

VIGNETTE

IT WAS A GRAND and glorious Hollywood occasion. We were to meet the visiting brass from New York City.

As a green country boy who never really got over his awe, gee-whizness and good goshness of anything at all to do with the entertainment industry, this was like—Holy Moses!

It's a good thing somebody mentioned that while it wasn't exactly formal—it wasn't exactly informal either.

Everybody came in uniform. Never saw so many dark blue suits, narrow ties, dazzling white shirts, well polished and burnished loafers. The cuff links were a thing of beauty.

I arrived at the sprawling Spanish type hostelry located somewhere in the backside evergreenery of Beverly Hills right on time. Just a hair early. Fifteen minutes.

I was met at the door by the top local vice president, who, not noted for his warm and friendly manner, outdid himself I thought in cryogenic courtesy. You could hear the ice falling on the floor in crystalline clarity.

It never occurred to me, sensitive fellow that I am, until several minutes later standing with a group of my fellows, that I was the only one there in a grey flannel suit, blue shirt and fire-engine red tie.

It was an evening of destiny.

As we stood joshing amongst ourselves in this more or less same group I had joined—or more accurately had joined me as on-timers and belated arrivers—a man approached. Very pleasant in appearance, friendly in manner, well dressed but rather carelessly so. "Good evening," he said, "I'm so and so, first and last name." I stuck out my hand and said, "I'm Dave Showalter from Hollywood. Where are you from Mr. So and So?" "New York," he said.

Realizing I had stuck my foot in my mouth, I dropped to the floor, salaamed, and said, "Glad to have met you, Mr. So and So."

He was of course the president of the full network, who immediately put this gauche country boy at ease by saying the salaam was a stunt he used on occasion to pick up a check when some guest refused to allow him to do so.

I did meet the New York vice president the party was held for—a man whose name I see today on my television screen in the very top credits listed. He traded me his red suspenders for my red tie.

The New York brass to an evergreen country boy was okeh.

The Hollywood brass was a different color.

One group of brass could listen and hear, without wallowing in the cliches of dress, protocol, and pecking orders. Which brass "got there"? Which brass communicated? Which was heard and heeded? One guess.

4

OK. So I'm Listening
I'm Listening! To What?

—*To everybody you can*, as a matter of simple, practical fact.

To the attitudes of others, their prejudices, hangups, no-no's, no-go's, things to avoid or overcome, positive points to be included in your presentation, knowledge and information relevant to the subject, and all the sources of fact you can personally dig up and glean from others.

At this point in time, you are going to begin to prepare to, "Use whatever signal at hand, in order to relate specifically to whomever you are addressing yourself, in such fashion so as to secure some kind of definitive action. Preferably in your favor."
—*Get somebody to do something you want them to do.*

With the factors in mind we have discussed, you are now going to listen with the same purpose, but with a different specific in mind. For good measure, let's throw in another maxim.

A GOOD COMMUNICATOR IS A GOOD RESEARCHER

By now, I am sure, from your own experience, and from some of the aspects of communicating we have examined, it is abundantly evident that there is a great deal more to good communication than simply opening the mouth. There is evidence to the contrary that some don't think so.

The thorough, complete and precise collection of fact, data and information, as a preparation for communication can not be overemphasized, for some reasons we will discuss later in detail on the dynamics of presentation.

In terms of *do listen* we pay attention to the man who knows what he is talking about. The more he knows what he is talking about the more we listen. The more we listen the more we hear and retain. Q.E.D. — *quod erat demonstrandum,* as Miss Fiditch my old math teacher was fond of saying—the better chance we have of winning the audience over in our favor.

Stepping up to a rostrum, or making a presentation of any kind, is an *unknown.* For all concerned. The communicator. The subject. The audience.

What will take place in basic action and reaction between communicator and audience is rather quickly determined in a comparatively short period of time. Action and reaction on the subject matter takes a much longer period of time. The first few moments are extremely critical for the communicator. So much for him is dependent on so many factors. How he looks. How he moves. His attitude. What he says. The credibility of what he says. How he says it. And so on.

During this exercise, however, we want to look at the *what he says* and *credibility* part of it, and its preparation. If we have

OK. SO I'M LISTENING! TO WHAT? 51

moved to the podium now in whatever form it may take, and have managed to avoid the errors we have mentioned, the next steps will, in great part be dependent upon what we have developed factually to back up what we have to say. This is not only important to your audience—it is of vital importance to you, in terms of staying in direct communication with them, in constant touch with them, not losing them someplace along the way, and for another very practical and helpful reason to you. Other than the essential credibility factor.

Communicators—actors, speakers, on-their-feet-performers in any circumstance—suffer the tortures of the damned prior to, and sometimes even into, the performance.

But, if you know your subject thoroughly, know that you know it because you have been personally involved in its research, data and information collection and its organization for presentation, it gives you two vital parts of communicating success. *Confidence and authority.*

That's a nice pair to draw to—and a practical guarantee you will draw another ace. Ease or comfortability of presentation.

This is tremendously important to a speaker. Any uncomfortableness, unease or malaise on the part of the communicator to the point that it becomes obvious to the audience, can be detracting, distracting and disastrous. The basic and only way to avoid that part of the unease, is to be thoroughly prepared.

Any speaker or stand-up performer, if he is any good at all *will* be nervous, apprehensive, worried, suffering the wim wams, and in some cases be literally physically sick. For those who think that such affliction is unique for them, or because of lack of experience and not at all experienced by the professionals—take heart. For good, expert, outstanding communicators, those who have been on their feet and in front of an audience countless times, this pre-speaking discomfort is as often as the number of those countless times, and as recurrent as the next time.

No communicator worthy of the name gets on his feet coldly, calmly and coolly, suffering no pre-play panic. If he does, you're in for a long and dull afternoon. He may look as if he is calm, cool and collected, but you can be sure, with the exception listed above, he is inwardly a kind of quaking mass, and outwardly trembling physically from the adrenalin shot into his system to help him cope with the emergency that faces him.

The communicator, like the successful athlete, is simply keyed to the top of his pitch, to his peak performance. Once he takes the plunge, the psychic and physical symptoms vanish in doing the job at hand. They can, and do however, return if the performance lags, goofs up, shows signs of failure, or indicates in any way, shape or manner that the communicator is not in command and control.

The actor, once he is past that much-anticipated yet almost dreaded first appearance on stage, relies on training and experience; on his ability to translate his lines into a communication with his audience that wrings from them every emotional response the play intends. If the play is bad; any part of it weak or inadequate; if cues are missed or do not come where they should; if the timing is off; if other actors in the play upon whom he depends perform miserably, the whole thing can go to pieces in short order.

The same is basically true of any performance.

In this specialized listening process, necessary as the next step preparatory to that one you take to the center of the platform, we are researching (listening) for information, knowledge and fact, directly related to and in support of the project at hand.

OK, SO I'M LISTENING! TO WHAT? 53

It might as well be considered listening even though it involves books, articles, pencil and paper, typewriter, interviews, conversation and observation. In its end result we listen to our compilation of all that material, assessing and organizing it in terms of how the audience will hear it, and hear it best.

Once we have researched the subject, and have organized it for presentation, we come to another absolute requisite for effective communication.

A good communicator is a good rehearser

In the armed forces it is training. Basic, advanced, specialized, whatever. In athletics it is practice. In any stand-up performance in front of an audience, it is rehearsal. However or whatever you call it, it all adds up to *doing over and over and over again* what you know you're going to have to do when the balloon goes up.

Along with knowing our facts then, our lines, instrument, weapon, game, job, profession, specialty or function, it is imperative that we practice or work at it if we are going to be good at it.

Even more directly than that, as any member of any combat team would attest, the ability to make even the first move, when your blood has turned to water, is almost totally dependent upon the disciplined reaction to a given command and situation that has been *trained/practiced/rehearsed* to the finely honed point where reaction is as automatic as it can possibly be. Otherwise we would never take the first step.

Communication, though different in function and degree, is no different in principle.

Communicators would do much better—formal presentation, sales pitch, training session—if they were to rehearse their presentation thoroughly. That means from beginning to end. Several times. Practicing diligently the use of any audio/visual aids they plan to use.

Two very important means that carry us through when the going gets rough, or the communicating function threatens to fail completely are—fact and rehearsal. The communicator who knows what he is talking about, and who has practiced what he is going to talk about, has that most important factor to all of us to rely on—something familiar, friendly and known, in the face of something unfamiliar, sometimes unfriendly and usually unknown.

Practice can't be relied on to make perfect, not at this time of world. But it can be relied on to make possible. Practice does something else too. Sometimes it makes "lucky", and you turn out to the astonishment of everyone, particularly yourself, the hit of the show. So practice and sing out. Don't fret if at first you get a little wet from the critical downpour. The winds are warm. They dry you off. I know.

And Then At Last You Will Succeed

VIGNETTE

IT HAD BEEN A LONG and tiring day.

One hundred or so Naval Air Cadets were becoming restive, awaiting their turn to rehearse. It was the NAVCAD Choir, sitting about midway up in the Hollywood Bowl watching the proceedings.

The Los Angeles Symphony Orchestra had rehearsed. So had a famous Chorale, for whom I have never had any liking since. Their conductor had carried them at least a half hour into the rehearsal time set aside for the even more famous baritone, the star of the Easter Sunrise program for the following morning.

It was obvious that an explosion was brewing. To say that the baritone was disturbed is a mild understatement. As producer for the event I was concerned, but most of all about the 100 young men, good and true, for whom I felt a personal responsibility. I had heard them at Pensacola. I had contacted them and secured permission for their participation for their first time appearance in the Bowl. They had flown across the country to be there and sing on that Easter morn—a not inconsiderable feat of logistics, rearrangement of red tape and public service.

As I sat uneasily with them in the close to 90° heat I said on an impulse from nowheresville to their Lieutenant jg director, "Lieutenant, if you and your men will hang on just a little longer I will guarantee to get you down there on stage in the shortest time possible, and jump into the pool in front of the stage fully clothed in the bargain."

A cheer went up from the men just about the time the baritone walked offstage, out of the bowl and to all intents and purposes right out of the program. I don't know whether he thought the cheer was for or against him. At any rate he disappeared—a problem to be dealt with later. The Chorale wore on for about fifteen minutes, then stopped.

Down the aisles charged the NAVCADs, running after the idiot who had promised the poolside performance. Up onto the stage, just long enough to shed my shoes, and into the center of the lily-filled pool I went.

As I rose to the surface, rocketing over the top of my head came the figure of the Lieutenant (jg) Director, not about to be outdone by some civilian.

We clambered out together, and he set his rehearsal in motion—a rehearsal that had something in it of a gleeful and glorious vitality that carried over to the next morning in a rafter-ringing resonance—the hit of the Easter program.

Oh, the baritone returned and sang. So did the Chorale. But the NAVCADs—they were something else.

The dividends of Practice plus that little something extra: Enthusiasm.

5

Beginning Middle and End

A GOOD COMMUNICATOR IS A GOOD STORYTELLER

He/she can be a writer, photographer, artist, singer, actor, dancer, cameraman, sound technician, editor, speaker, politician, husband, wife, can in fact be anyone who has a need to communicate with somebody else.

The need, as we have discussed it, is much more profound, much deeper seated, than we give it credence. We need to communicate to survive. Materially by all means, but spiritually as well.

A hopeless alcoholic, skid-row inhabitant, down-at-heels, broken in body and spirit, a brilliant career and mind destroyed, speech blurred and unintelligible by the illness which had beset him, mumbling for a tape recorded documentary momentarily shook off the fog enveloping him and said something very plainly with an infinite sadness and pathos I have never forgotten. "It's the loneliness," he said, "It's the *loneliness*."

Our need to communicate is at the very fount of life. Its difficulty in doing so is evident on all fronts. Our inadequacy in face of this necessity is not only frustrating, it is sometimes appalling to us, and sometimes actually destroying.

Assuming that we have gone through the preceding pages without giving up, we have arrived at the place, the unavoidable point where, if we are going to communicate effectively, we must needs get our material together in some kind of communicable fashion, which then, if delivered capably will secure action for us. In our favor.

Schools of journalism have taught their students a practically infallible formula for getting the facts for a story. Their graduates have been using this formula successfully for years, cascading it from that base into a variety of that part of the storytelling art that would probably bury most of the inhabitants of the earth under an avalanche of paper, film and tape.

Who, what, when, where, why, and how, is as good a start for a beginning, middle and end as you will ever find. Nobody has yet improved upon it, and it is doubtful, as a matter of fact, that anybody ever will as long as communication as we know it and its concomitant storytelling art exists.

If we were to change our style of communication overnight to some kind of sending and receiving by osmosis, omnivision or fingertip manipulation, that is probably what we would want to know anyhow. I doubt if even the computer will change this means of informational output—or outformational input. Don't knock it. That may be the next step down the road.

In organizing material for any kind of presentation the five W's and an H are not only valid and helpful in putting it all together once you have secured it, it is equally valuable as a

BEGINNING MIDDLE AND END 61

guideline for research. Inevitably unless the presentation is comparatively simple you will find it necessary to go back to answer one of these W questions to complete your story. They are a kind of *nag* in a way that won't let you rest—until all the blank spaces are filled in.

Actually this information gathering technique obtains for every communicating technique from a memo to a motion picture. Not so much detail in a memo—although there is no reason why it couldn't be more informative—and a raft of detail in a movie, a book, or any more complex communicating effort. It is directly applicable, for example, to preparing material for a training session, a sales pitch, the conduct of a seminar or conference, a speech, audio/visual aids of all description—or a speech to the PTA.

Complete fact gathering within this peripatetic perimeter does not guarantee you can write the story well, but it does say, if you organize your material with that definition in mind, you will be able to put a story together that is logical, factual and that has continuity. Better, incidentally, than you might consider yourself capable of doing.

The other certain side of the coin is that if you don't organize your material by this dictate you can be equally sure it won't be much of a story.

Every story must have a beginning, a middle and an end. It must start someplace—preferably with an interesting beginning. It must proceed someplace—in logical support. It must conclude someplace—as a result of.

It helps if it is concise, coherent, cogent, complete and comprehensive. It must be told so that so far as possible all can understand, although I do not necessarily agree with those who insist that words should always be simple or no more than two or at most three syllables. Storytelling is intended to be *chal-*

lenging and *stimulating* as well as informative, factual and logical. While it is certainly advisable to keep it simple so that all do understand, it is also commendable and recommended that you put some spice and color into it however you find it fits your style.

Storytelling can be as simple or as many faceted as the situation sets the scene for. It can run the gamut of expression, drama and emotion. From your standpoint as a kind of specialized communicator, it should use all the means at hand for spinning its encapsulating web—the spoken word, the written word, the pictorialized word, any combination of the above that best serves to: imprint, record, pictorialize, in a fashion that secures action in your favor.

How in the world do we go about doing that?

We begin, once again, by listening. Genuinely listening. Listening for the purposes we have already outlined. Not listening at that point for an opportunity to display our knowledge, intelligence or *14-karat* personality. Listening by asking questions that secure answers within that who, what, when, where, why and how technique. Listening to really hear what is being said, even though you may disagree with it totally.

We do it by research and study. All possible information, pro and con. We do it by formal organization of the material—usually on paper. We do it by *commitment*—selecting the approach, the story-line, the means/method to be employed in telling the story. There are as many different ways of telling a story as there are storytellers. Each one of us tells even the same story differently than somebody else—that blessed individuality we own!

Once we have garnered all our facts and information, an important essential is to *make the choice and then stick with it.* Indecisiveness on this score breeds inaction, and in the end result not much of a story. Interestingly enough once you have made the decision on the route you will take, the way opens before you rather simply.

Some of the factors that need to be taken into consideration in this commitment are; what is it you want to achieve or accomplish? With whom? What are its plusses? What are its handicaps? What is the best way to tell the story? What are the circumstances in which the storytelling will locate itself?

Now that you have marshalled a squad to an army of facts—depending on the scope of your communicating project—the next thing to do is *get it on paper*.

Nothing organizes so well, or perhaps it is more accurate to say nothing organizes you better than the cold, hard necessity of getting the whole *megillah* on paper. In apple pie order. As hard and difficult work as it is there is no other way to go. Being a story man myself (*my one prejudice in this entire presentation I think!*) I am inclined to think that the story is of principal importance.

While I am on that bias I feel quite strongly that anyone faced with the necessity of getting on his feet and making some kind of communicating presentation to an audience would simplify his task if he viewed it as a storytelling process—organizing his material that way and then delivering it in the same psychology or philosophy.

It isn't really much different than telling a funny story to a group of people. Communicator, subject, audience. The need to take center stage all by yourself—"Look Ma, no hands!"—with no help or assist from anyone. A group of people who may range from good friends to acquaintances to potential and actual enemies. You are on your own. As a matter of fact you have signalled that intention, served as your own emcee or chairman

64   *HOW TO SAY IT SO THEY HEAR IT*

of the day or event. The group is willing to give you the opportunity or take a chance on you. All eyes are on you. You begin with an introduction, which establishes the circumstance, follow with middling and establishing detail, and finish with a belly laugh of a punchline.

During the course of this short storytelling procedure—maybe a minute or two in duration—you have used dramatic expression, inflection, gestures, looked every member of the audience in the eye, reacted to them, milked it, timed it profssionally, and have been an outstanding success.

Why? To begin with, probably because you had confidence in the fact that you could do it and not fall flat on your face in the process. You knew the story from beginning to end, all its detail, innuendo and implication. It is a favorite story of yours. You have told it many times, knew what the reaction would be and that it and you would be successful. (*Applause!*)

We might run back through it just for the fun of it to see what axioms, maxims, rules, regulations, suggestions, hopes and prayers of communication were involved.

First off you took the risk and plunged in with the realization that it might be a real bomb. Secondly, you treated your audience like ordinary, regular, human beings, assuming they would enjoy the story. Third, to the best of your histrionic ability you used the tools of the trade at hand. Fourth you did your homework, and incidentally got in some more practice. There are some other things included here—listening, researching, rehearsing, presentation dynamics—but let's don't belabor the point.

Making a speech, telling a bunch of guys how to do something like keep their fingers out of the machinery, making an annual report or a presentation to a board of directors, teaching, instructing, or using sign language, is now and forever will be *storytelling.*

A speech, a formal presentation is like telling a joke. Expanded. Frequently literally true, unfortunately, because the communicator did such a bad job of it. Seriously, in truth, it is a kind of expansion of telling that joke you did so well. Apply that kind of psychology or practical thinking to any kind of presentation you are faced with. It should be helpful.

Let's look at some other aspects of this terrific story you just laid on the group.

Maybe you didn't originate it, write it, or put it together but if it was a successful story, you can be sure it was well put together in the first place, and if you were to break it down would contain all of the material organizing elements of the basic who, what, when, where, why and how.

Another facet of it, essential to good story organization and writing, is the fact that its author also put it through a careful process of editing, a process probably employed by other storytellers enroute to your usage of it. You probably edited it somewhat to fit your own delivery or capability.

All of which simply illustrates, (1), the need for putting it down on paper in the first place—organizing it, and (2), the need for editing it—paring it down, expanding it, rewriting it, adapting it to your own style—prior to presentation.

A GOOD COMMUNICATOR IS A GOOD EDITOR

I can also guarantee that before you opened your mouth to tell the story you ran over it in your mind at least once, to make sure you had it down pat, particularly any tricky or difficult part of it. Once you were fairly certain you had it all in hand, you cut loose. Maybe a matter of seconds in your last run-through, but run through it you did—and better—do.

The same is true of any *on-your-feet, in-front-of-an audience* presentation. The same process, basically that is, in greater detail, involving more work. The same successful result is there, and in direct ratio to something we discussed some time back—the amount we are willing to invest, to risk, of ourselves in the communicating effort.

We are afraid to stand up in front of people and communicate. Stop right there. We are indeed. *Afraid.* It is an absolutely normal experience and reaction, essential, as a matter of fact, if we are to perform well on our feet.

We are afraid we won't do well. We are afraid we can't do it at all. We are afraid we will make a spectacle, an ass, a laughingstock, of ourselves. We are afraid we won't remember what it was we were going to say. We are afraid of failure, and we aren't about to do that! Let alone run the risk of it in front of all those people.

The protection, and as close to any guarantee of anything you'll ever get for not failing in that circumstance, is *preparation, rehearsal and work.*

I am sorry to say, boys and girls of communicationland, there is no excuse, absolutely none, for making a poor on your feet presentation in front of a group. There is even less excuse for any top representative of any corporate body to get on his feet and do a miserable to middling job of making a speech. Although many do.

If we do, and I am also sorry to say it is universally applicable, it means in simple words that we have failed to consider our audience as simple, fallible human beings, just as willing to consider and accept us as communicator in the same light, and we have failed to do our homework. In that case, as you can easily see, we failed before we got on our feet, and its result. although too bad, is a certainty.

But there are also those happier times. We get to our feet, anxious, doubting, with a sense of goshawful doom. And we win the house, or the vote, or the silver medal for impromptu oratory because we rehearsed in advance the right thing to say at the right time to say it. We *think* about the audience. *What* does it want to hear? *What* should it hear? Then we speak up. And they listen.

"Never Mind the Cold."

VIGNETTE

WE TOOK A BUNCH TO ALASKA, to Elmendorf, Ladd and Eielson Air Force Bases to entertain the troops.

It was a memorable occasion from any point of view. The talent ran from top-notch to ordinary—some of it perhaps even less than that, but one thing for sure it was a big-hearted and fun bunch of people with one thing in mind. Do a good show for the guys.

One person always stands out in my mind on that stint, and interestingly enough turned out to be a kind of hit of the show although entertaining as such was not his forte. He had been a favorite of mine for years, and his efforts on that trip did nothing to dim that lustre.

I had done an interview with him for the network, and had, on impulse, explained the nature of the project, and then, somewhat hesitantly asked him if he would like to go along.

"When do we leave," he said.

So it was set that he would be part of the troupe, accompanied by his wife as part of the bargain. Both of these charming, wonderful, gracious people were in their seventies. He was concerned immediately about what he could do or say that would be of any entertainment value to the troops, or indeed that any of them would even know who he was.

There is a saying in Alaska that you are a greenhorn until you have urinated in the Yukon, wrestled with a bear and slept with an Eskimo woman—or words to that effect. In four letter words it comes off rather basically.

A very popular pop singer opened the program. An equally popular Western style balladeer closed it. Both very attractive gals. The performer in question was placed about midway in the show by the director (who I was sure thought I had rocks in my head for including this gentleman as part of the troupe), so that any sag in the rock and sock of the thing could be quickly picked up.

There was no need to be concerned.

When he was introduced to that audience of thousands in the first show at Elmendorf, lean, lank, silver-maned, his first words were, "I've spit in the Yukon, wrestled with an Eskimo. Where's the bear?" And then went on to talk about Hollywood and the Lux Theater in which he was then starring.

His name? Otto Kruger, longtime dramatic actor, second lead and heavy in the movies. A favorite of mine, and certainly a favorite of those three air bases who recognized an old pro when they saw one.

They heard Otto because he had first heard them. He did his homework. And it was cold up north that year. But it was warmer for the guys because of a professional with a heart and a thinking head to back it.

6

The Dynamics of Good, On Your Feet Presentation

The time has come now for you to be a stand-up performer. Up to this point we have basically explored and discussed the mechanics of the communicating art. Those factors both essential and helpful to you for the now imminent curtain call.

As a lead-in to a perhaps rather surprising first in the area of presentation dynamics, permit me to tell you about two experiences which stand out in my mind as illustrative of the pre-play panic most of us experience.

The first, my speech at my high school graduation way back in the dim past. I got on my feet, absolutely petrified in front of that unbelievably, to me, massive and frightening audience, got the first two or three sentences out and went completely blank.

There just isn't any blanker feeling in the world. For what seemed like minutes to me I stood there holding my ground, waiting for the next sentence to come back out of orbit. It did. I proceeded, finished my speech and sat down to a kind of ovation. Not because of the speech or its stylish delivery—but because I simply hung in and didn't quit. Before you consider affording me any undue credit just let me tell you honestly I couldn't think of anything else to do. I'll tell you something else. *I've never made a speech from memory since.*

The second memorable occasion occurred several years later as I stood in the wings to make an entrance on stage, balancing a saucer and a cup of tea in my trembling hands. This was *penthouse presentation*, and you could hear it rattle both on and offstage, if not right out into the street, caught up as I was in a plain case of sheer terror.

I am sure you have heard of actors, performers, athletes, so severely afflicted by this uncontrollable physical and psychic circumstance that some have actually become ill and vomited prior to the performance. Not all individuals suffer that traumatically, but once again let me reiterate—most of us do suffer to a painful degree of one kind or another.

Now we come to a different consideration of it. It is not only a natural reaction, it is an essential and required dynamic of effective personal presentation, like it or not. First of all it means you are emotionally involved. That takes in a lot of territory. It means you are interested, excited, enthusiastic, keyed up, on edge, worried, fearful, apprehensive, concerned—everything, in short, every good performer, every capable performer, every winning performer, brings to the starting line every time he goes to the mark.

Primarily, I suppose it relates to the fact that we want to do a good job, and are afraid we won't. Therefore we call up everything within our power to make sure we don't fail the issue.

I would be much more worried and immediately concerned if I didn't go through that fearful and apprehensive (*nervous*, if you don't like the terminology of it) state prior to speaking in front of a group. As a matter of fact I would be certain that I was sick, or that there was something indeed wrong with me if I didn't feel like that, and that I was in no state to make a speech. In its ultimate definition—that is right. I would be, in that circumstance, in no state to make a speech. *An effective speech.*

This painful emotional involvement spurs us on, keeps us on our toes, keeps us alert, aware, responsive, builds a continuing and unbroken line of action and reaction, two-way sending and receiving with the audience.

Without it the communicator is *dead, deadly—and Dullsville.*

Professionals, in whatever field may be theirs, can move into the next sequence, drawing perhaps on years of experience; fully developed capabilities as communicators; even perhaps on unusual charisma, personality, wit or intelligence—and not need to go so far into the necessity for preparation and rehearsal you and I find necessary.

Remember. I said not so far as. I know of no real professional speaker, actor, entertainer, performer or athlete who doesn't prepare and rehearse. (Train and practice.)

After that first blinding burst of speed springs us from those starting blocks, we need the wind, stamina, physical condition and will to win to get us there. As a communicator it affords us an ease of manner, a comfortability, that makes it possible for us to overcome that prior unease and malaise, and then to employ all those dynamics of effective personal presentation.

COMPONENTS OF EFFECTIVE COMMUNICATION

Enthusiasm

Enthusiasm, while part of emotional involvement, is worth some special attention of its own. If one had to choose one element alone in using whatever signal one had a hand, *et cetera, et cetera, et cetera,* enthusiasm would top the list.

The least equipped amongst us, however that might spell out—illiterate, not able to write as well as others, maybe not a personality kid, possibly handicapped in some fashion—can carry the day in obvious, genuine, effervescent, outgoing, contagious enthusiasm. His speech, in terms of mechanics and dynamics may be far from the greatest, but his enthusiasm makes up for and outweighs any obvious lack or inadequacy in communicating techniques.

But, don't count on enthusiasm solely now that we have emphasized it so favorably. Just include it. Homework for you can place that jewel of enthusiasm in the setting of communicating beauty and workmanship it belongs and deserves.

Integrity

Another dynamic of good communication could be called the verities, or perhaps, integrity.

We've already talked about phony or counterfeit as highly undesirable content for any presentation we have in mind. Things such as truth, honesty, genuineness, sincerity, however you care to characterize it are absolutely essential to good communication. It means your product is valid, has character and integrity. It makes the sale worthwhile, easier and renewable. It builds confidence and reputation.

Inflection

What about inflection or gestures? They certainly aid and abet communication, although they are not an absolute by any means.

All of us have endured at one time or another the unflaggingly repetitive, monotone with which some speakers endow their effort. Since the age of onsight television and its incursion by so many salesmen, from politics to philosophy, we have also become aware of the inhibited, chopping hand motions or the no motion or movement at all used by some speakers. Such usages either awkwardly emphasize or provide no emphasis at all for points. Sometimes, as a matter of fact, we become so fascinated with the gestures that we miss the facts.

Inflection or gestures, while not a necessary requirement of good communication, can be extremely helpful—if they are normal, *natural, not overdone,* overpostured or overplayed. What a thing of beauty and joy it is to experience a speaker, a lecturer, an on his feet point-maker, or storyteller of any description, playing that communicating instrument like a virtuoso. Whose voice rises and falls like the tide—with an accompanying volume register from a whisper to a crackling thunderstorm. Whose entire body is in tune to the tone of the speaker, subject and audience, and whose every movement is as fluid and graceful as a wandlike willow in a spring breeze. Or, who by the slightest movement, glance or nothing more than an eye movement of inference, conveys the full implication of the accompanying and spoken word of the moment.

Such talents help keep the speech alive, vibrant, interesting, moving and freeflowing—and certainly assist in helping you *secure the action in your favor.*

Word Usage

How about word usage? *How about that!* Simple and understandable by all you bet. Geared to the group to whom you are addressing yourself, by all means. But, once again with some qualifications for your consideration.

There is no earthly reason—despite the purists and experts—within the basic context suggested above, why words that can be understood by their relation with, or proximity to, other words or within the meaning of a sentence, can not be used even though their meaning as a word may not be understood by all. Even the most primitive of audiences like to be complimented to that extent, like to be considered as capable of understanding something more than the monosyllabic A B C of it. All of us are the possessors of pride, ego and vanity, and I suggest you use some word frosting, if you believe in it, and if it suits or fits you. I believe it will improve your communicating ability and effort. It extends you a little. It extends your audience a little. That has some valuable communicating worth all its own.

It relates, I suppose, to a kind of taken for granted thesis, the validity of which I suspect, question and challenge—the idea which one area of the communicating business is generally credited for and uses, that the average mentality in these United States is 12-year-old. I consider that a condescending, tolerating, crock of pickles, and suggest that you as a communicator label that one, put it in a jar and place it on the shelf out of reach.

If there are words or terms that need definition—define them. If slang or colloquiallisms helps—use it.

Attitude

If we were to define one part of the dynamics of communication as *attitude*—you might consider these suggestions.

Include, embrace, encompass your complete audience, from opening to closing word. Look at all of them. Turn your head, as you speak, so that at one time or another you have included, are including, your total audience. Look directly at them, eye to eye. Establish and keep contact with them.

Talk to your audience, never at or down to them. Speak simply. Speak slowly and succinctly. Articulate plainly. Watch for and be aware of audience reaction, and respond to it. Keep within the specified time limit. The old show business axiom is a good one. *Leave 'em laughing or leave 'em wanting more.*

Use humor where it fits naturally. This has some real plusses and a handicap or two. In its natural, uncontrived state—humor or jokes that relate well and fit in smoothly, the ability to respond humorously to an ad lib situation, lively, sparkling wit—such usage can be a real assist, extremely helpful and audience winning in almost any communicating situation. Exceptions of course are those occasions where, for whatever the reason, humor is in bad taste.

A caution extended earlier to you about off color jokes or *blue* material—unless that is what your audience is expecting of you—as, for example, a stand-up comedian in a night club.

In formal communicating—speech, lecture, sales pitch, seminar, conference—you are better off not to use anything of questionable nature at all. If something gives you pause to consider at all, don't use it. It can downgrade, denigrate, and in fact, destroy your presentation, its effect and its result. *Believe it or not*, this is true. It may offend one, some, several, and even on occasion all, of your audience. I am not talking about stuffy, stilted or inhibited speeches. I am talking about plain, common, practical sense, what works well in communication and what does not. If it is offensive, or possibly so in your feeling or estimation—pass it.

HOW MUCH HUMOR?

A further word about humor generally. You can inform and entertain very effectively and with much to be desired result. There is, however, a *fine line* where comedy overwhelms straight lines, and the serious import of your communicating effort goes by the board. In short you have to determine whether you are going to be a straight man, employing some illustrative humor or a comedian.

I cite you the case of a political leader of a state, a very capable, very talented, very fine man, who found this a career-changing problem. He was a charming, intelligent, interesting, dedicated, personable and fine individual. He was, however, not believable in his chair of political leadership because he couldn't resist the temptation to entertain. He was a premier raconteur, storyteller par excellence and could compete with any stand-up comedian in the business. But he was not a comedian. He was a political leader. The use of humor is particularly tricky for anybody in the public eye as a political leader. We have a habit of expecting our heads of state to be serious, responsible, problem-centered, certainly not un-humorous, men, but with little time for anything but the business at hand, which is usually anything but funny. The business of administering the affairs of the people is a serious business, and we expect it to be conducted that way.

In our own communicating efforts this is another essential dynamic to remember. We have all sat in audiences where the speaker's effectiveness on the serious subject at hand suffered, because of an overbalance of humorous content.

This is not to say at all that comedians haven't got a serious bone in their body, or are incapable of serious thought, or are not possessed of much in the way of intelligence. *Far from it!* This attitude, completely unwarranted and unjustified, is the greatest cross they have to bear.

My friendship and acquaintanceship with some of them has dramatically demonstrated to me that they are among our most intelligent, intellectual, sensitive and understanding people. They have a remarkable ability to relate to people—at the people level

—a no withholding willingness to give of themselves in the *risk* position we talked about earlier. Their contribution is a much needed and welcome relief to the everyday humdrum, the tragedy and pathos that is part of life.

No. We are simply saying that natural, well planned and timed humor is extremely useful in any formal, serious presentation, and that beyond that we have to make a choice—comic or straight man.

PARTICIPATION

The primary goal or objective of any communicator can probably best be specified as *participation*. In the degree of participation is the touchstone for the action we are attempting to secure in our favor. In the participation you secure as a communicator you will find the prime mover and the basic learning process you have been seeking.

Everything we have done in preparation up to this point directs itself, cognizantly or not, towards participation. The communicator himself is participating. The more he recognizably participates in all of the areas we have discussed, the more his audience participates.

Success in communication comes in direct ratio to participation. And participation is usually a matter of *wanting* to participate on your audience's terms as well as your own. Whether the audience is five thousand paid ticket holders, or one lone cowpoke.

80 HOW TO SAY IT SO THEY HEAR IT

The Many Splendored "Yep"

VIGNETTE

WE USED TO SEE THEM, Gary Cooper, his wife and daughter, believe it or not, on a rather remote stretch of public beach down Malibu way, real early of a Sunday morning. Before the crowd turned out in force.

A surprising circumstance, and certainly an enjoyable one, as we sat quietly by not wishing to intrude or in any way make a move that would flush this prize quarry.

He came out of the water on that morning as I was about to enter and do some body-surfing.

I was hoping I could think of something to say befitting the occasion, or that I could indeed say something at all without sounding like some inane and complete idiot, and yet not wanting in any way to intrude upon the private life of this very famous Western hero, noted as a quiet, shy and rather uncommunicative man off screen as well as on.

"Kinda chilly," I blurted out.

"Yep," he said, "Ain't got much paddin'."

Communication doesn't always require a lot of words. "Yep" can say it all; and if a few more syllables are added, they put icing on the cake. One more thought: Participation is a two-way street, not "should be", but "has to be."

7

The Name of the Game

Communication is participation.

Its best result comes, or is secured, when you as the communicator or sender, participate. When you do you become emotionally involved. When you become emotionally involved you perform at peak powers. When you perform at peak powers you send a message—*tell a story*—that is alive, vibrant, energetic, electrifying, enthusiastic, action packed, crackling and charged with power.

Its reaction comes when the audience or receiver participates—and that degree of participation is almost totally dependent upon you, although the feeling is mutual once underway.

Even the subject becomes part of the participating means if we follow the lead suggested in earlier chapters. Material fully researched and well rehearsed gives you a friendly and familiar tool to work with. The dynamics of presentation you are able to employ lend color, life and interest to the subject matter. Assisting aids—blackboard, flip chart, color slides, motion pictures—extend, expand and pictorially dramatize your presentation.

All of it has a single objective. *Communication.* Participation. A decision in your favor.

There is no subject, including the traditional *motherhood* that does not have two sides to it. For and against. Yes and no. If it were all a one-way street communication would be simple and life equally dull. Any *communicator*, from the *husband* attempting to convince his wife, to the *negotiators* at the peace talk table, is or should be, aware of this. Since communicating is a people problem it has people handicaps.

Two sides to every question is only the beginning. Each side has numerous supporting viewpoints. In considering the people problem—something every communicator must or should do to assess his chances of success or failure—we, for purposes of simplification, can probably divide it into three categories. 1. People who can't hear you. 2. People who are willing to listen. 3. People who hear you very well.

PEOPLE WHO—

Can't Hear You

We have all experienced this, usually on a one to one basis. Somebody with whom we instantaneously, automatically, lock horns. It is a frustration. It is disturbing, upsetting, maddening. Worse than that, in a group communicating situation such an individual can confuse, obfuscate and roadblock the issue so effectively that it can become impossible of resolution.

THE NAME OF THE GAME 85

No matter what we say to one another in this circumstance, we can't hear each other. We have already made up our minds and nothing the opposition says—valid, factual, irrefutable as it may be logically—is going to change anything. As a communicator we must recognize this as a fact of life, that one, some, a majority, and sometimes all, of an audience, to all intents and purposes can't hear us.

They listen to the extent of using the points we have made as turnarounds for them, or they listen long enough to either interrupt or take up where we leave off—but they really do not hear a word we say. They don't want to.

One-to-one disagreement is difficult enough. One-to-several can be catastrophic. Some examples of total audience turn-off could be: a known and recognized *communist* speaking to a conference of FBI personnel; a *bigot* speaking to the American Civil Liberties Union; a *racist* talking to blacks.

Will Listen

In any group or audience with the exceptions, and others similar to those listed above, there are people willing to listen even though they may basically differ with your viewpoint. They comprise those who, like you the communicator *(I hope)*, recognize that there are two sides to every story, and on that reasonable, fair minded basis, are willing to hear what you have to say. They may still not agree with you in terms of a decision in your favor, usually for very good reasons of their own which can be communicated equally effectively in opposition. It is important to keep this in mind in any kind of communicating procedure for reasons we will discuss shortly.

Hear You Very Well

This part of an audience is already in agreement with you, already on your side, believes what you say, is in accord with it.

They affirm, add to, extend and expand their knowledge, belief and experience as they listen to you.

Now, let's go back a bit.

HOW DO THEY HEAR YOU?

People basically hear what they want to or need to hear, however that want or need defines itself. That definition probably comes from a complex of factors that could be generally delineated as prenatal influence, family relationship, upbringing, education, training, experience, social and job status, income, living conditions and so on. Simply stated, relevantly and viably viewed from your standpoint as a communicator, it is the unique, individual imprimatur we have emphasized so strongly—*your own individual fingerprint.*

The next thing essential to remember is that people, generally speaking, hear things subjectively. How it applies to them. How it affects them. What it will or will not do for them. Individually, self-relatedly. Also, they hear how it applies to others within the capability of their own interpretation. How it works for them first. How it works for others second. How it works for you as I see how it works for you—which may not be, probably isn't, accurate at all.

We hear then, *subjectively, self-relatedly.* The cave and survival is only a few short steps back down the road, regardless of what some would have us believe, and that basic instinct is a prime factor and fact of life. We hear personally, individually and emotionally. We hear in direct terms of how it affects our survival. Survival today, admittedly, is different in a thousand fragmented frangipani ways, but it is still, survival.

At the risk of becoming involved in a battle of semantics I suggest that any communicator should consider that man also makes his decisions emotionally. If, for this purpose, those who disagree can grant that the thinking process is physiologically an emotional process and therefore such techniques as analysis, evaluation of facts, logic *et al,* are then all part of the decision making process, we can, for this outing, stay in stroke together.

However, I doubt that possibility, recognize the validity of the two-sided premise, and therefore make my position clear.

I believe that decision making is at the same gut level and visceral level as communication; that it is neither head nor heart, but is something more like the unexplainable mystique that surrounds man and finds such terms as soul and spirit so difficult, if not impossible, to describe or define. I believe that man makes his decisions emotionally. I suggest he is *apt* to make his decisions emotionally. I further suggest that you and I as communicators better accept it as a practical fact of life, *get on with the job and leave the argument to someone else.*

Everything we have said here—most of it about the audience—has its direct application to us as communicators. We need to be able to recognize, as best we can, our own *individuality, potential, problems and hangups.* We must know and recognize that the side we are presenting is one side, although we believe it to be factually, logically, honestly and fairly presented, taking the other side into consideration as well. We need to hear at least as well as our audience, and perhaps we would do well to caution ourselves that we need to hear *better* than our audience.

PROBLEMS TO AVOID

Let's look at us for a moment or two as communicators, and specify some further problems we face, perhaps defined as personal or attitudinal roadblocks.

While it can easily come under the heading of obvious, the farther down the communicating roadway I go the more I realize that there is absolutely nothing that is obvious. Further, sometimes the simplest and most important points you fail to make are those you didn't—because they seemed so obvious. We got on the edge of it several pages back in talking about immediate, practically on sight reaction to someone for no explainable reason. And in that instance there really isn't much we can do to change that mutual image.

We can however, look at some specifics, personal or attitudinal, where we, by taking action ourselves, can avoid some problems in the communicating process that work in our disfavor.

Personal appearance is a *prime factor* in any kind of personal presentation. It is amazing, for example, how spinach between your teeth can discount a speech, a kiss or an application for a job.

The only real point I am going to make about personal appearance at this place in our discussion is a very basic one, within which you can set your own requirement.

Don't let your personal appearance work against you or the communicating project you are going to present. In this you have a very selfish, vested, personal, surviving interest. *Success versus failure. Winning or losing.* Doing the best you know how to do, and knowing that is exactly what you did.

Personal appearance needs to fit the mode and the mood of the audience. So does attitude.

We need to be very careful, for example, that we come across as the genuine article. Of course, the easiest way to manage that, is to be just exactly that. But we need to exercise care that we do not register as conceited, supercilious, condescending, know it all, tolerant, sophisticated, privileged, ignorant, insensitive, unkind, unfair, unprincipled, immoral, immature—any negative that takes us out of, above, or below, the range of our audience.

The inclusion of *tolerant* or *tolerance*, may surprise you in this group. I suggest however, it really says to its listener, "I find it necessary to tolerate you." His, my, your, immediate reply is, "What for?" *Or more colorful.* We may as well close the conversation at that point. We have effectively closed a door between two individuals.

YOUR SUBJECT

The subject matter, the intermediate part of this three piece communicating symphony, plays an equally important role along with the communicator and the audience.

Its theme can sometimes cancel you out completely, no matter how expertly you communicate. "White Supremacy" at a meeting of the NAACP. "Black Power" at a KKK rostrum. "Democracy—The Only Way" in front of the Soviet Politburo.

If we go back to the three classifications—people who can't hear you; people who are willing to listen; and people who hear you very well, we can make a point about subject matter and preparation of vital importance to any communicator.

First of all—*a suggested axiom.* Make your presentation factual, fair, accurate, straightforward, honest, and insofar as possible, without error in any fact, quote or reference you use.

Write that in black and white someplace just to re-emphasize it, or somebody may write it in blood for you.

Your only hope of changing any mind, attitude or idea of a group from whom you have already been excluded without so much as opening your mouth, is that your subject matter has been immaculately, assiduously prepared on exactly the foundation I have suggested above. The only protection you have against being pilloried and crucified—and having it stick—is by adhering to that basic formula. Nothing pleases an oppositon so much as to be able to catch you off base, with facts, figures, statements, inferences.

Your chances with that segment of an audience that is willing to listen, albeit opposed to your position, are only as good or as bad as the words you issue within or outside that perimeter.

Your affirmation and support from those who are already on your side, is strengthened with that kind of presentation, and weakened with anything less than that.

We are great believers in fairness and fairplay. Not necessarily because of any altruistic motive on our part, but practically speaking because fair play from somebody else for us depends on its use with others.

Whatever its philosophical base I suggest it as the only route to go in effective, perpetuating communication. Once again, for a number of very practical reasons. It is usually, almost universally, recognized as such even by your most vocal, irreversible opposition. It is recognized as such by those in the audience who have the potential of becoming an ally. It confirms your position further for those who are already in agreement with you. It is unassailable on anything but an unfair basis by the opposition, or it is assailable only on a fair basis by the opposition. It establishes you in listeners' minds as a communicator who tells the story like it is. It establishes a reputation for you as a communicator with character, honesty, integrity.

I might suggest in conclusion of this chapter's discussion the employment of the following to help establish an *attitude-set* as a kind of infallible operational base for any kind of communicating effort.

Consider yourself a guest in the house.

Think of yourself in this light whether you have been invited to make a speech, or have, in effect a captive audience, an in-company presentation to employees. A captive audience needs to be captivated.

You are a guest, with all its intended and extended courtesies and implications. Time has been set aside for you. Considerable effort has been expended in your behalf, not only to make the time available, but in all the mechanics as well that go into arranging a meeting. People have gone out of their way to tend to these details and set them in motion—all for you. People have made themselves, their time, and their facilities available to you. You will be accorded all of this deferential treatment, all of these efforts, all of these courtesies, without a murmur of protest or a ripple in the lake of decorum even should your stay as a guest in that house be something less than desirable.

I am mindful of Sunday dinner, as a boy in the home of my grandparents in eastern Washington. It was seldom without guests, as I remember. The occasion was *for* the guests. The whole family, the house, the affair and all its accoutrements, were the servants and the means for the event. Guests were center stage, the cynosure of all eyes, the object of all attention. If a guest accidentally knocked over a glass of water, was guilty of some malapropism, the perpetrator of a social faux pas or the possessor of a noticeable peccadillo, it was graciously dismissed, covered up or overlooked—whatever the occasion demanded.

Guests, on the other hand, were equally aware of their position and responsibility. They frequently came armed with gifts, flowers, candy. They went out of their way to be of no burden or imposition. They extended themselves in conversation, in politeness and the social graces.

Making a speech or presentation should be no different than that. Certainly, viewed in that light it can be extremely helpful to the communicator in establishing an attitude incomparable in its approach to effecting a fully participating circumstance.

That, my friends, is communication. Be a guest in the house.

There's a corollary expression: "When in Rome." There are houses and there are houses. Being a guest can mean not soiling the towels. It can also mean disrobing and buffing it at midnight in the heated swimming pool. And sometimes it can mean not getting in the way until the smoke clears. Remember it's their house, not yours; and it is sophomorish to be sniffy about things you don't understand completely. There is nothing in the bylaws that says being a guest is a placid voyage on a gravy train. To communicate, be a guest; which means adapt quickly and be ready. For anything.

94 HOW TO SAY IT SO THEY HEAR IT

Waiting it out with the C.O. or Second-Guesting a General

THE GENERAL WAS LOADED. Who knows why or how come? Maybe too many tough command decisions. Maybe he just liked the juice.

He invited us to tour the base with him. We jumped in his car. He pulled up first at fighter base headquarters. We walked in and over to the desk. A couple of sergeants were laboring away at Sunday morning tedium. "Morning Sergeant," the General said. "This is Mr. Showalter and Mr. Tracy from ——" and he named the network.

The Sergeant was just barely civil, enough in lapse to anger the General, who, in civilian garb and without his stars and full Air Force regalia, looked almost as squarely unmilitary as we did. It was obvious the Sergeant didn't recognize him. It was equally obvious that unless you knew the General well it would have been difficult to recognize him.

It was also obvious to the General. "Scramble!," he said. The Sergeant completely aghast, said, "I beg your pardon?"

"I said Scramble," the General repeated in short, clipped emphasis.

The Sergeant, caught in that paralyzing vacuum of the unbelievable versus the just barely possible believable, was between a rock and a hard place. "I'm sorry sir, I can't just order a scramble. On whose orders sir?"

"The Commanding General of this base, and it's too bad when its personnel doesn't recognize its general. We'll have to do something about getting you people shaped up down here."

At that critical point a Captain appeared on the scene, took the whole drama in in one glance, and completely devoid of any expression or emotion, nodded affirmation to the Sergeant, who posthaste hit the Scramble button.

"Come on," said the General. "Let's go watch it from the control tower."

He stalked out. We followed close on his heels, caught up in a small crisis that had to run its course. We pulled up at the gate to the control tower guarded by a couple of armed PFC's. We were immediately challenged. Once again it looked as if we were going to run aground, but a hollered command from the control tower stopped that developing emergency. Up the stairs we went and into the control room area where everybody snapped to in unison. "At ease," the General said, stepping back to observe the mission.

Two jet fighters, in answer to the Scramble had taken off, run the practice exercise, and were ready to set down. As they made the pass over the field, preparatory to breaking off into a landing pattern, word came over the intercom from one of them, "No green light on the board. Landing gear not in the lock position."

I wished silently at this point we had not stopped in to see my favorite General.

It got quiet and tight in the control room. The intercom was busy with questions and suggestions. The first jet sat down and got out of the way. The second jet flew over the field, gear down. From a command and observation position out on the runway, the report came in that the gear appeared to be locked. The word was relayed to the pilot.

"Okeh," he said, "I'm coming in."

He made a long, wide, thundering circle, and began his approach in an equally long and flat glide, as flat as he could make it without stalling out.

The fire engines and other crash gear were waiting for him about a quarter of the way downfield. For some reason all the sound around us seemed to diminish into an almost audible silence. The General stood as immobile as ever, not an expression on his face.

The fighter greased it in, popped his chute and began his run-out. The crash and fire trucks revved up and rolled. The jet ran on down the runway—safely.

There was a great, gusty sigh of relief. Everybody began to breath again.

The General looked at us and smiled. Then he said, "Let's go have a—cup of coffee."

The coffee could have lubricated a B-36. We played the game. We drank it. What, if anything, was learned that day? If the General says "Scramble," they do; even if the General is higher than the planes. It's a better system than the opposite. Saying: "We'll scramble when you pass the sobriety test, Sir, and when we feel like it." Generals have their off days too, but they are still Generals, and it's their job. Being a guest is remembering, even when it irks, that they are still Generals.

8

Smoke Signals

It is interesting to note, when we have been invited to be that house guest we signalled out with in the foregoing chapter, how frequently we miss a rather unusual opportunity.

It is a rather unusual opportunity you know, although apparently not considered much in that exact frame of reference. Communicating with a group is indeed and in truth not only an unusual but *rather remarkable opportunity*.

Let's say, for the purpose of discussion, that we have learned all the lessons of the previous chapters, and some of our own; are capable at this point by dint of application, hard work, practice and some luck of doing a good job as a standup performer in front of an audience.

PRESENTATION AIDS

To this guest appearance are you planning to bring a box of candy? A bouquet of flowers? A specially handicrafted gift of some kind that bears your own recognizable signature, and individual imprimatur, and by which you will be long remembered and appreciated? If so, *congratulations!* You have just won a box of candy bars—and don't call us, we'll call you!

There are several assisting presentation aids, not only helpful to you, but worth putting to work. Again, for several various and practical reasons. The opportunity, frequently overlooked, is the employment of all the means practicable, to secure the participation we talked about in the previous chapter. Particularly when it relates to smaller groups of say, forty or less. (No hard and fast rule about the forty. Just no more than you can manage in the kind of participating action we are going to explore.) Our prime objective, as always, is that *individual*, who, sold singly, one by one, adds up to majorities.

Perhaps the term *audio/visual* is misunderstood. Its usage is sometimes overdone. It is more often than not however, not used at all; not effectively used; and sometimes so misused as to practically cancel out what otherwise might have been a good communicating performance.

There is no substitute for, nothing so effective as, personal presentation, for reasons so impassable and as simple as the individual factor we have been emphasizing. There are, however, very helpful sales assisting aids which punctuate, underline and perpetuate the personal presentation.

We need to be careful in their usage that we do not allow ourselves to be overwhelmed by the sheer and dazzling technocracy of an exquisite array of a sophisticated complex of machines. Practically anything you desire in any single or composite instrument you like, is available for audio/visual purpose. We are a great people for gadgetry. The one basic caution I would issue is that we do not become so overcome by the fascinating ease with which something works or is supposed to work, that we overlook its practical, efficient and applicable function.

Directly allied to this is the fact that you do not necessarily have to invest a small fortune as a first step in this direction. Look first towards what is already available and at hand, and which is within the capacity of the individual who is going to use it.

Let's go back and see if there is any validity, use, purpose or profit at all, in any kind of investment in time, talent, personnel or money, in this secondary and supporting communicating role and function.

At any sales, training, educational, informational, orientation meeting, where any one or a combination of individuals is selling an idea, project, plan or method, *the whole purpose is communication.* The results obtained are totally dependent upon effective communication. (Not just there, incidentally, but on down the line.)

In its simplest essence, as suggested earlier, real communication is, in turn totally dependent on participation. Participation in terms of reaction and action, enthusiasm, interest, acceptance, rejection, criticism, evaluation, analysis and discussion. Anything but sitting on hands. Something that means and underscores the simple, observable fact that your audience is awake, listening and learning.

As a matter of further observation let's extend the business of communicating a little further. Communication *is* participation *is* learning.

Part of our responsibility as a communicator is to develop this sensitivity to, and awareness of, our audience. With a big audience the sensitive, responsive, participating communicator observes, records and acts differently than the communicator to the small group.

He sees it in nods of affirmation, in smiles, in overt body movement, in alert attention to what he is saying, in obvious awareness of what he is saying, in sometimes nothing other than seeming blank and no response attention—but nonetheless attention, in applause, in any of those genuine expressions of appreciation, affirmation, commendation or opposition that an audience affords its communicator.

Those are participating signals our audience records for us as certainly as a seismograph records an earthquake. Rejection as well as acceptance is as identifiable as the face or movement of your audience. Keep in mind, also, as a suggestion, that rejection is participation too, and as a matter of fact can be just as usable by a competent communicator as acceptance. It can be challenging, stimulating, thought-provoking, crystallizing and resolving, provided you, accept it that way, know what you are talking about, and accept it in good part without, if possible, getting angry or uptight.

SMALL GROUP PARTICIPATION

While we are at that specific area, let's talk for a few moments about the dynamics of participation in front of a small direct action group, where you expect a result in the way of doing something specific as a follow-up to your presentation.

Just as we do in front of a large group, we need to put everything we have considered and discussed up to this point to work. We need to know our subject thoroughly. We need to know every facet of it. We need to be thoroughly rehearsed in its presentation. We need to be able to call upon all of our communicating ability. We need, least of all at this point, to be some kind of *know-it-all* with all the answers. We need most of all to approach it on the individual, human being, non-labelling principle we established as the first and most important precept of effective communication.

In some of the less generalized requirements and more specific areas of dynamics in this small group participating presentation, where the communicator and his audience are going to be directly involved with each other in what amounts to a discussion leader and question and answer basis, we need to develop certain capabilities.

Establish Give and Take

Like or develop a liking for give and take, close-up contact, infighting, footwork and confrontation.

This is not necessarily a talent you have to be endowed with. Like almost anything it can be learned and acquired. Since communicating itself requires that we move out of a circle of inactive, passive, introverted, introspective, contemplative, immobile non-risk, into its reverse adjectived opposite and position of risk, it would seem to follow that any one of us who sets out and learns to be a specialist in communication could effectively manage the above requirement.

Probably generally true. But it takes involvement in doing it. You have to try it to find out. It takes practice, experience and infinite patience.

It has some indescribably satisfying rewards in terms of personal achievement; achievement in concert with a group; a continuous learning process of your own, only accomplished I am convinced at this level of involvement, and finally an indestructible feeling and awareness of the individual, his individuality and his oneness with others as we communicate, participate and learn together.

Take Charge; Keep Charge

Stay in a position of leadership, without stifling question, probe, criticism, evaluation, analysis, and sometimes just plain insubordination, rebellion and rejection.

This takes some doing. It relates somewhat to the factors we hae considered above, as I am sure you will recognize. But I believe it can be wrapped up in a kind of homely truism, which, if you were to shoot full of holes in theory, you would still find comparatively waterproof in action.

Basically, as an attitude, it defines as being willing to risk yourself and your product, as best you know and accept yourself and it to be. Included in that willingness is the simple recognition that you are fallible, subject to error, quick and humble to admit it, and observably as eager to learn as those with whom you are risking yourself.

This is somehow or other a recognizable attitude that registers to observers without wearing a neon sign that lights up and says it is so.

It says a lot of things to a lot of people without formal proclamation. Particularly as you act it out. It says you have come to know and accept yourself. It says you are willing to lay your knowledge, experience, ego and pride on the line. It says you are concerned about, but not afraid of, challenge, and that you know and accept it as a vital and integral part of the learning process. It says that you beleve communication to be a three way system—sender, subject, receiver—with active participation as its *modus operandi*.

It sends a message, loud and clear, which more simply says something like, "Here I am in a position of leadership. I think I can manage it and am willing to earn and prove its validity." Once that position of leadership is accorded you, that is just exactly what you continuously do, earn it and prove it.

In front of a large group of people you achieve this in a kind of lecture process, with sometimes no opportunity at all, or a very limited one at most, for free swinging interplay between speaker and audience. How *well* you conduct yourself as a communicator at that podium is the determinant of your position as leader.

With a large audience you manage that position of leadership accorded you, by displaying all of those attributes of good communication we have discussed. One of the penalties we pay for slipshod preparation and presentation, is not just delivering a poor speech, but something far more critical, vital and important— loss of status as a leader. It's one of the best reasons I can think of why anyone in a position of responsibility should be an excellent communicator.

Within a small group the attrition can become painful. With you as an authority on a subject in front of a group of established, or would be authorities, it can become not only painful but deadly. In a group with a *sharpshooter* or *expert rifleman* in the audience who squeezes off a shot wherever and whenever a target appears, it can be disruptive and disturbing to the point of chaos. In a group where what can only be described as a *mouth-off*, having no claim to any expertise, incontinently puts in his oar, it can be just plain disaster.

With that small group, however, lies not only our biggest communicating challenge but best opportunity to participate, learn and get the job cracking.

Perhaps the best answer to the all important issue of maintaining that position of leadership, other than by assertion of despotic authority, is found in the next specification and its pursuant suggested guidelines.

Keep to the Issue

Know how to keep the question on the issue at hand and return the discussion unerringly to that issue when it gets untracked. To do this we need to know our subject backward and forward, upside down and inside out. It is our last resort when everything else fails.

We must believe totally in our subject. Any serious crack in this mother lode can develop into a chasm.

If we don't know the answer to a question posed, say so. If somebody else has the answer let him say so. If nobody has it, get it and come back with it. If there is no time for that, say you are sorry and get on to the next point. If you guess at it or blatantly answer it knowing you are or may be wrong you can get caught so flatfooted you will forever have fallen arches in front of that same group.

Don't get so uptight or emotional about your subject that your reaction to a question or comment is anger—particularly anger directed towards an individual. Anger towards a situation is understandable and acceptable. Anger towards an individual even though understandable is not acceptable. It can lose him as well as part of, and sometimes all of the audience.

Also, remember that good communication does not come only from agreement. It also derives from disagreement. There are two, and in fact, many sides to any subject. One man's position is as good as another's, including yours. Don't just let or allow, encourage the expression of opinion, but keep it within the perimeter of the subject at hand, and return it to that position when it untracks. In fact, with the sharpshooter, expert rifleman or authority, who usually have valid points to make, this process will expand and enrich the learning process. It lends color, vitality, vigor, authenticating data, and frequently keystones added input from others in the audience.

This does not apply, however, to the *mouth-off,* the self-appointed expert or pseudo authority—bless their pea and nit pickin' hearts and little old pointy heads. Given time—particularly in a cohesive group that knows each other—his own peers will eventually take care of him. This is the best possible solution. Unfortunately it doesn't work like that often, so there you are with at best a very uneasy situation on your hands. The bane, incidentally, of stand-up comedians or night club performers is the heckler, mouthoff or smartoff, usually inebriated as well to bolster his attack.

The next best way to control this situation is to get back to the subject. Turn the situation back to the subject, *repeat, back to the subject.* You, however, must hear this individual out at least once—long enough, so that, you can assess the situation; and equally important because you will need them as allies, his fellows and associates can do ditto. You can't just close him down prior to that first runthrough, not only for the above stated essentials which accomplish something very useful to you—but also because any arbitrary, first blush, inconsiderate closeout can serve to hinder and impede the communicating mode you are striving to achieve.

This, as any stand-up performer soon learns and comes to know full well, is a trial and error situation. There is no pat way of handling it except to use patience, restraint and courtesy however you mount the counter attack. In the end result you may have to close him out beyond question of further interruption on his part. By that time the group will be aligned with you and the closeout on your part at this point will probably become obligatory and mandatory from the group standpoint.

This is a command decision, and it does affect your position of leadership, and I suggest simply, that at this point you take action dad, whatever you deem necessary. Like, shut him down!

Questions and Answers

By question and answer, demonstration and illustration, let the audience draw its own conclusion and perform its own learning process.

For the accomplished communicator, the question and answer approach, however you decide to conduct it, and with whatever means you decide to employ is where the excitement, action—and fun are.

Remember too that this is a basic storytelling process, with a beginning, middle and end, and directed towards some facts, points and conclusions that you want demonstrated. Preferably in your favor. In simple, hard, practical fact you have already researched, developed, organized, written, rehearsed and produced the story—or somebody has—for you to present.

Personal, on your feet, stand-up performance is the key to it and the biggest part of it. Enter, however, at this point, those assisting audio/visual aids we have been hinting at and touting for some wordage now.

We will deal specifically with this frequently missed, misused and misunderstood opportunity shortly, but right now let's emphasize, their audio/visual desirability as extremely effective helpers, and the need to know what to use and how to use them.

What you are really doing in this assisting audio/visual aid process, is, recreating a story you already know and want told, getting it created (re-created and re-told) by the very audience you want it told to. In that participating creation, you establish the best learning process extant, taking an active, individual part in the origination and development of the storytelling vehicle itself, and, use the audio/visual aids to underscore and imprint the story.

The story told in this fashion, if it is well written and all that implies, will pretty well hold its basic storyline. It will, however, expand, delineate in further detail, fact, color, interest, drama and effectiveness from the contributions of each storyteller in the audience. It can also, in this participating context, uncover points that had not been envisioned, open new avenues of thought and experience, and even in some instances change a storyline for the better.

Summarizations

Summarize conclusions drawn from the participating communicating process in such fashion as to record, imprint and perpetuate them in the listeners' minds as effectively as possible.

The only comment here is that this is extremely important by both on-sight presentation via several audio/visual means, and paralleling confirmation of it with supporting printed data in the hands of each individual in the audience.

Action

Convert the presentation and its conclusions into as practical and profitable plan of action, corporate and individual, as soon as can be devised.

This is essential to do and implement as quickly as possible. Nothing is deader, costlier, more wasteful of time, talent and money than resolution without ensuing action.

CONCLUSIONS

OK. These are six basic guidelines and comments for small group presentation, employing the principle that involves the communicator and his audience in active, action-producing, risk-involving, indivdual and group participation.

Incidentally, talking about *fun* reminds me to suggest that fun as such, should be, and is, a definite part of good communication, rather than just plain, unrelieved, deadly serious action. Even that, in the following context, and the real point I would like to make, can be—fun!

Years ago I was accorded an important, and to me, interesting promotion and assignment. In discussing it on the way home with an associate and official of higher rank in the company, I said in all sincerity and enthusiasm, "It's going to be fun!"

Shock, horror and disbelief registered on his face. "Fun?," he said, "You mean work don't you?"

I meant exactly what I said. The work was going to be fun.

You can read it any way you like but I seriously suggest to you that communicating-participating-learning, as we are discussing it, not only is, but can be, fun as well as work.

A frequent and traditional last admonishment by an unusually harried, worried and apprehensive director, as a cast of actors waits backstage on opening night in the expectant hush before curtain time, is "Have fun!"

It is sound communicating advice.

There are those occasions, of course, when "having fun" becomes an awesome challenge to the pilgrim spirit, those cheerful occasions of storm and stress that contrive to try men's souls. And that's when "having fun" is really "Fun!"

VIGNETTE

WE HAD BEEN ALOFT since seven o'clock that morning. We took off from McClelland Air Force Base near Sacramento in a WB-29, on a weather mission flown regularly from that area, up into the Gulf of Alaska, over towards Hawaii, and back home. About 3,000 miles of continuous flight. I was doing a documentary for the network.

What woke me up was some comment I heard vaguely, like, "We're socked in here. We'll have to try someplace else. I sat up from where I had been snoozing—directly over the exit hatch where the cold air seeping through had kept me wakeful anyhow. I sat up on the step leading to the cockpit of the WB-29, behind the pilot and co-pilot and listened to the conversation.

The pilot had one of those flip page maps in his lap looking at the alternatives. And voicing them. Home base was socked in. Matter of fact the whole Sacramento Valley was. Victorville was open. Not bad. Close to home for me.

It was about 11:30 p.m. We had been dropping from 18,500 feet, the altitude at which we hit the California coast, cold and crystal clear—about 32° below outside—and were presently at 9,000 feet. The skies stretched away endlessly, CAVU—ceiling and view unlimited. Beneath us was a fluffy cotton blanket.

The conversation in the cockpit was fascinating.

"How about Hamilton?" "Nope." "Let's try the San Francisco peninsula. Might be able to get down at the Oakland Navy Base." "Ever land at Oakland?" "Not me. I'm new out here."

I've landed at Oakland, and am not fond of it. Matter of fact I don't care much for landing anywhere in the San Francisco Bay area. Particularly in the junk.

The lights of San Francisco, a gentle glow in the murk through which we were flying, showed beneath us. An occasional break in the fog revealed the city, peaceful, unaware, desirable, so near and yet so far away.

We flew on down the Peninsula to around the San Jose area, turned and headed back north towards the Oakland Navy Base. On our way back we flew over two fields. Each time the conversation went something like,—"Is that Oakland?" "I don't think so." Even I knew it wasn't Oakland!

It didn't do much to help my chickenhearted civilian security.

"There it is," the Major said.

Ahead of us, dimly discernible, at the low altitude and out of the heavy fog overhead, was a long string of landing lights stretched out in beckoning welcome.

I hadn't moved from my position since I first awoke, except to edge closer forward towards the pilots in my effort to help them land the giant aircraft successfully. With a rumble and a thump the wheels came down, then the flaps, and we began to buffet about slightly as the WB-29 began its probe towards its mother element.

The landing lights came closer. Suddenly the aircraft veered from left to right, the engines roared. "Christ," the pilot said, "I missed the runway."

With that I turned my back on the cockpit, and waited for the worst. "The hell with 'em," I said to myself. "Let 'em land the goddam thing themselves."

We touched down, seemed to run out forever and finally braked to a stop.

The mission was over. It was midnight. I was pooped.

I dumped my several days laundry out in the utility room for rehabilitation, if not rest, upon my return. "What is that?" my wife said. "That is the landing at Oakland, and shut up!"

This poignant reminiscence reminds me of two lines by a champion communicator named Ring Lardner: "Are you lost daddy I arsked tenderly. Shut up he explained." Indubitably, one may aver that sometimes there is no more succinct explanation.

9

Will Somebody Flip the Switch, Please?

What kind of audio/visual aids for what purpose?

Communication, according to our definition, means "using whatever signal we have at hand, in order to relate specifically to whomever we are addressing ourselves, in such fashion so as to secure some kind of definitive action. Preferably in our favor." *Getting somebody to do something we want them to.*

It can be relatively simple. Raised eyebrows and a shrug. A wink and a smile. A touch and a sigh—or a slap!

Communication does not depend on words. Words frequently confuse the issue. "I should never have opened my mouth." "When you open your mouth you get in trouble." "I didn't understand a word he said." These are frequent and valid complaints.

Communication, the prime mover of life if you will, can not be inactive and inanimate. Like its partner—life—communication is risk, risk involving and risk taking, unless you're never going to get out of bed.

It would be interesting to know how much of the communicating process between individuals is managed without words at all. Some have suggested an approximate sixty per cent. I have no scientific knowledge of my own that confirms that wonderful old Chinese proverb, *"One picture worth ten thousand words,"* or any of the present day statistics that tend to confirm this ancient observation. As a communicator professionally involved in communicating I know that pictures work. Word pictures and picture pictures. A well balanced combination of the two works best.

There is a picture we paint for each other that is a fascinating one to contemplate, and one I submit to you for consideration, as the simplest and most basic of the audio/visual tools at hand. Immediately and already available, and I doubt if considered in that assisting aid, light.

VISUAL IMPRESSIONS—BODY LANGUAGE!

You. Your body. Without opening your mouth. What you wear. How you look, your posture, your attitude, without saying a word. It is a visual impression of us that has an immediate, accurate, indelible, elephant like memory, sometimes almost irreversible imprint, as others see and hear us, establishing a kind of conditioned response that can be helpful, favorable, positive or handicapping, unfavorable or negative.

What we are shows. Some outward indication of the inner and real man, strangely enough usually a rather accurate index

WILL SOMEBODY FLIP THE SWITCH PLEASE? 119

is apparent. Not always, not totally, not without exception and error, but still a rather honest picture of an individual and certainly a readily observable one. One to which we definitely react.

Let's start out without words first. How do you assess an individual at first meeting? By looking at him. A quick once over, probably both instinctual and learned, perhaps even reaching back to more primitive times when the need to know enemy from friend in the shortest possible order as the balance maybe between life and death.

If we think about it a little, we probably learn it at the earliest possible moment that we become cognizant and aware of our surroundings and the threat contained therein. As little nippers finding out quickly as a self protective device that mother and dad responded painfully to a situation in direct relation to an observable posture, attitude, body movement. Words weren't necessary. We knew the sky was about to fall in on us. Words usually accompanied it, but we got the message way ahead of the vocal onslaught; we learned it early and words were nowhere near as painful as the action.

It is an instinct or learned capability that we use constantly in every kind of individually relating and communicating function; that we put to work for us early in life; that becomes a part of memorable, useful and practical life experience; that we call on constantly, subconsciously without any seeming effort, or consciously, to help us assess a situation, an individual or a problem that can be inimical to us.

As we have come along then, in our own unique life experience, we continued to learn to read what the man was really saying even though the voice we heard in all its blandishment was in direct contrapuntal accompaniment to what we knew was true.

This should give us some clue to that puzzling situation where we have to assess the difference between what it sounds like the man is saying, and what we know by other body signs is not the case at all. It is sometimes difficult and confusing to read. The body says one thing. The voice, another. *Which does one believe?* Unless the two are in obvious concert we tend to believe the visual evidence we see in the body movement. That's where the moment of truth is, from long and painful experience.

In our first and basic usage of a visual aid then, as a communicator, or communication in toto, the suggestion should be that we do not promulgate, promote or sell something to somebody unless we fully believe it, believe in it, and know it worthy of support. Otherwise someplace along the line our body is not going to accompany our voice, and with that obvious split in our communicating procedure the audience splits also. They may still be there but nobody will be listening.

AN OUTSTANDING EXAMPLE

As the best example of the finest audio/visual presentation I have ever seen, let me interject for a few moments a personal experience which demonstrates the values I would like to discuss.

In instructing classes regularly on the techniques of defensive driving, I am first of all grateful I do not have to conduct the eight hour course solely by lecture technique. I am sure the participants would agree. Before that, I appreciate fully and thoroughly all the storytelling technique, we have discussed here, that Chris Imhoff, creator and organizer of the National Safety Council's copyrighted course, used in putting this incomparable story together.

Secondly, it is a real teaching assist in this remarkable communicating process, to have a magnetized blackboard and model cars to demonstrate traffic safety problems and answers; a set of

WILL SOMEBODY FLIP THE SWITCH PLEASE? 121

similarly magnetized captions, headings and definitions printed on cards also for use on the blackboard; a colorful printed flip chart for referential, factual and point making support; a set of eight 16mm color motion pictures for illustrative expansion, direct action demonstration and full color support of each lesson's subject matter.

At the teaching podium in front of me, I have an instructor's manual, complete with all information relevant and applicable to the subject. This is not just an ordinary manual. It is put together in a three-ring binder much like a movie or television script Information on the subject matter is printed in sections down the right hand three-quarters of the page. Cues and directions for the use of audio/visual aids are printed down the remaining one-quarter left side of the page. The instructor's manual, handsomely and colorfully bound is constructed to fold in such fashion as to provide its own lectern if one is not available.

Third, it is easy to see and observe the reaction of the participating class to this simple but comprehensive communicating process—watch them as they respond to it. It obviously helps induce and stimulate lots of action and interest. It punctuates and underlines the subject matter. It pictorializes, demonstrates and illustrates the traffic safety problem. It summarizes the material and draws its intended conclusions. It uses a 16mm color film with each lesson to make the problem as real as it can be short of being in an automobile on the road. It places in the hands of each participant comprehensive, illustrated support, reference and back-up in the form of a printed and bound student work book. As its finale it issues a certificate of appreciation and wallet sized graduation card.

Fourth, it is designed to be an active, individual and group participating, communicating process, at the learning level of self expression, involvement, risk, decision and action—the very meaning and implication of communication itself.

Its objective is much to be desired, totally and completely valid. *To save lives.* To reduce the number, severity and cost of traffic accidents. To help accomplish this by providing a competent, professional course of defensive driving instruction to be taught to every adult licensed driver it can enlist.

Its story line is factual, fully researched, substantiated and supported. It is set up and organized for the instructor, with specific as-you-go instructions, stage directions and cues. It is structured in palatable segments of approximately an hour's duration, that precede and follow each other in logical sequence and continuity. Each segment, though directly related fore and aft, is complete of itself.

Like any effective communicating process, it requires assiduous study and rehearsal on the part of its communicating representative. Like any effective communicating process it gives communicator, subject and audience full range exposure, participation, action and interaction, learning and applicable usage.

With such a well planned, written and produced audio/visual communicating process, detailed to a fine point, yet flexible in its presentation and audience participating conclusion and decision, any one with a basic interest in traffic safety could take the instructor training course and teach the subject competently, if he were to: study diligently; practice and rehearse fully; develop a store of knowledge of his own on the subject; stick close to the Instructor's Manual; use all the audio/visual support; and, teach regularly.

Its goal is heroic, its outreach ambitious but achievable. Two very basic requirements of effective communication. *A valid and worthwhile goal. An achievable goal.* Difficult but not impossible. Contrary to all the talk and humor on the subject, the *impossible* does not take a little longer. It takes forever. We do not do the impossible, and whoever set that incipient failure syndrome in motion, or stands in support of it, past, present or future, deserves the commendable fate of continuously demonstrating for us that he/they can indeed do the impossible.

So much for an outstanding communicating process. I recommend it to you for study and usage. It encompasses much of what we have discussed at some length on effective communicating generally, and is an outstanding example of the ways and means audio/visual presentation can be employed.

SIMPLE AIDS

However, a communicating program or process does not have to be as comprehensive as that, in terms of the audio/visual assists.

Felt pens, and some imaginative usage, can be very helpful. They, of course, can be used to letter on overhead projector transparencies or for blank page flip charts. You can use them for lettering headlines in combination, perhaps, with a typewritten presentation. You can use them, vari-colored, for your own speech outline and maybe on vari-colored paper stock separating major points by using different colors. This is a good device for you as a communicator, if only because you have made the presentation important enough in your mind to do something special about it.

A typewritten presentation, beginning with the five "W's" and "H" and employing the refined storytelling technique of proposal writing to sell a project, program or idea, is invaluable to an effective communicator. With today's electric typewriters and electronic copying processes; with a kind of artistry which can be accomplished with typewritten type faces; with the affirming, confirming, time for consideration at leisure, perpetuating and record keeping features this visual aid exemplifies, we should never fail to use it where it is practical to do so.

Don't overlook a blackboard, an eraser and some chalk. For the minor investment involved you can expect a major return, if you work at it. While you're at it you may as well get a portable magnetized blackboard and double its potential. You can still write on it with chalk. You can also use magnetized models, captions, headlines, to demonstrate problems, answers, action. You can produce your own illustrated flip chart. In color. With printed or lettered pages and illustrations. All you have to do is plan it, research it and write it. Somebody else can do the technical part of it for you. It isn't as expensive as you might think.

The overhead projector is a simple and useful aid. You can manage this with felt pen and cellophane transparencies, or have it done professionally by a commercial artist. A 35mm slide projector should be an integral and much used part of your communicating arsenal. It can be an excellent instructing, informational, training and orientation device. Once again it does not have to be expensive. You can readily learn to operate today's marvellous cameras, and the results you obtain in color can simply, dramatically and graphically illustrate points you want to make in your communicating process.

Motion pictures become somewhat more complex in terms of treatment, application, cost and usage, but you at least ought to have a motion picture projector available for showing films already produced that have application to a particular subject or problem. For the rest, it is a subject all of its own, and we won't deal with it here.

In any of these deployments of audio/visual aids you need to plan them very carefully. In that planning you might go back to those guidelines on research, writing, rehearsal, dynamics and presentation we have examined in some detail.

No discussion of audio/visual usage can overlook one of its most important pre-presentation requirements. You have been

WILL SOMEBODY FLIP THE SWITCH PLEASE? 125

present at meetings, I am sure, when the microphone went dead, the projection lamp (still and motion picture) burned out, the sound failed on the motion picture projector, or something vital and essential to the presentation failed to function. It is imperative that you are as well prepared for such snafu as you can possibly be. A specific check list would be useful.

You can employ these audio/visual aids singly, almost without any cost at all except effort—or in any kind of combination you find practicable, and at corresponding cost. You can, for example, employ a slide projector and tape machine, with your orientation or training story recorded on tape, with the two machines in electronic parallel and hook-up, turn the tape machine on, step back and sit down, watch and listen to your own presentation. An excellent teaching assist method where you have to tell the story over and over again.

You can run almost any combination of slide and motion picture projectors and tape machines you want on an electronically operated and programmed basis. The basic comment I have in this instance is:

1. Assess your own communicating need directly related to the problem you are going to tackle.

2. Determine whether audio/visual support is valid or not; what that audio/visual support should be; what of it is already available; what audio/visual aid best suits your need; what expense is involved and justified; who will handle the responsibility and what kind of special training or education may be necessary; and, exactly and specifically how it will be used, towards whom it will be directed and what is it intended to accomplish.

Audio/visual aids can be terrific. They can also be a *bomb—an undetonating dud* in one sense and an exploding fall-out in another that settles like a deadly pall over an otherwise successful communicating process.

Nevertheless I strongly recommend its usage wherever possible in your stand-up performance as a communicator. Every storyteller, worthy of the name, seeks those *Open Sesames* that enhance and improve his art, that aid and abet his chances for success, reputation, adulation and reward.

The story he has to tell, the talent, ability and hard work he employs in telling it and the means he uses to make that story perfection itself are his lifeline. Tenuous true, but also with great tensile strength.

Audio/visual aids are an integral part of this. They are some of the interweaving strands of his lifeline. No real storyteller will overlook them. As a matter of fact, he dare not.

Because that lifeline has to be kept intact and taut. When communication stops, or becomes stymied through ignorance, fear, the anger of poverty or even the isolation of wealth, then life eventually dries up and stops. Real storytellers can't overlook anything. They try to get through with all the tools available. They have to try.

Fatal But Possibly Not Painful

VIGNETTE

THERE HE WAS. IN PERSON. One of the world's richest men. A tycoon—as they say—of business and industry. Handsome, distinguished in appearance, reserved but courteous and personable. A name that anybody would recognize. A man with an international chain of establishments.

We had just finished a tape recording of his prepared speech for the network.

While there, I thought, what an opportunity to do an interview on tape. Where did he come from? How did he get his start? What was his education? What had he learned along the way? What was the key to his success? What were his failures? What did a man need to do to emulate him? What words of advice to young men?

There were some of the immediate questions that popped into my head—and of course, the coup it would be to have this exclusive interview for our listeners.

I explained what I had in mind, emphasizing its importance. The simplicity of an interview on tape. No problem should he find himself at a loss for words. Re-phrasing or re-statement of a question should he find it not to his liking. The fact that he could listen to it played back and ask us to exclude any portion of it. Not at all like a live interview where words once said stood as they were uttered and no opportunity for recall or elimination. He agreed although somewhat hesitantly.

We began with some opening and simple questions. He had a very difficult time expressing himself, to the point practically of being tongue-tied.

After a few moments of this I knew there was only one thing to do—as embarrassing as it might be. I thanked him very much for his courtesy and kindness, and quit. It had obviously not only been an embarrassing, but a painful experience to him. He left the studio in noticeable relief.

It has remained to me—as the King of Siam said on stage—a puzzlement. He read his prepared speech well. He certainly had the position, power, wealth, experience, background and training, far beyond even those in the very small percentage of people who become so eminently successful.

What then?

Was it just the microphone—an admittedly frightening mechanism to the uninitiated? Fear of the ad lib and not prepared statement? Worry about being quoted on something he perhaps shouldn't have said—without legal advice? Not really having anything of importance to say or afraid he wouldn't say it so it sounded important? One man talking to all those millions? Concern about how it might reflect commercially on his business?

All of that I am sure, and possibly this—

What about that supreme pinnacle of loneliness, experienced by those in the highest places, where people say what they think you want to hear, and you cannot really say to anybody what you not only want to, but need to, say. Almost desperately.

Perhaps he couldn't make the requisite sounds because he had forgotten how to listen, or the echoes around him provided a rigorous diet of nothing worth hearing. Could he ever remember what it was that he needed to say? A chronic case of broken lifeline due to aggravated non-communicationitis.

Yes, it can be contagious.

10

Promotion, Pay and Profit

WHAT IS IT GOING TO DO FOR ME?

A fair question. What do you want it to do for you? The beginning of a good answer. What indeed *do* you want communication to do for you?

Let's start out with a fact and necessity of life—making a profit. How about for a motivating theme, "How to get the job done with/through/by other people—profitably?"

With that as a kind of practical basis, may I suggest that you begin to look at *profit* in all its implications and meanings, and possibly some definition of it not otherwise surfaced or considered before. What are all the aspects, every single one of them, of the profit making function in your situation?

What does profit mean? It can mean the customer who has cancelled out an automobile manufacturer, not dissatisfied with the vehicle so much as with the dealer, whose service to the customer has been totally unsatisfactory. Does the irreparable loss of a customer who has invested $4,500 in an automobile and who will never buy another one of the same make, important?

What does profit mean? It can mean a worker injured on a job for any one of a number of reasons, that could have by preventive action of some specific description saved the company time loss, production hang-up, insurance costs, personnel replacement and training. That represents profit that was never achieved. Multiply it a little across a big industry payroll and it can get to be pretty interesting.

What does profit mean? It can mean that somebody failed to specify clearly and unequivocally a goal, an objective, a means and a valid reason to attain it, or a simple job and someplace between the administrative, supervisory and functional level, the word not only got mislaid—it was never found!

What does profit mean? From a corporate standpoint it can mean that the profit goal, objective, motive, means, was rather clearly understood, specified, required and even commanded—but profit for the corporation did not necessarily mean profit for the individual employee.

What does profit mean? For that individual employee? We might begin by asking him, as a kind of intelligent and practical starting point. It doesn't necessarily have to mean sharing in the company profit as such—although a number of companies are finding that a very effective practical consideration. It doesn't necessarily mean either, money or peripheral benefits—although both have some extremely useful application. It means both of these considerations certainly, if a company can find itself capable

PROMOTION, PAY AND PROFIT 135

of managing it. Most important, however, and nobody can really specify to what degree, is the simple factor of, inclusion.

Profit is not just the possession and goal of the corporate structure and its stockholders. It also should have some basic meaning, implication and motivation for the individual employee. What does profit for the corporation include in it, for example, for the employee? What is its meaning for him besides a job, a position, a responsibility, promotion, wage, salary or even bonus?

Inclusion in, being part of, belonging to, participating in, a group, along with the individual imprimatur, might just as well be considered and included in the basic functions and needs of life. They can hardly be ignored. After the fact of existence and survival, they become of prime importance.

I am not talking about some kind of soft-headed intellectualism or wild-eyed radicalism. I am talking about a very basic, practical principle, one we overlook constantly and fail to implement regularly.

What kind of inclusion are you inviting—not just allowing, lip-servicing, tolerating or condescending to or extending to—but inviting from employees? So he's dirty and stained from hard work. He has grease under his fingernails. He don't speak too good and ain't the greatest intellect in the world. He lives in another world. You wouldn't, don't need to, he doesn't want you to, spend a moment with him socially. He has a beer with the boys. You have a cocktail at the club. He doesn't expect to be the same as you. No sir. He is different and he damn well wants to maintain that difference. So do you. So should both of you.

Whoever has been feeding us that pap about the equality of man, has got his nurture nipples mixed. Man is by no means equal, nor is his status.

He is the same in one respect in that he is a fellow-member of the genus homo sapiens, an associate and dues-paying full member of the human race. He is the same in both his similarity and his complete distinction as a unique individual. He has been said to be *equal*, created so. I believe that to be unrealistic, impractical, unachievable, impossible and inhuman.

At the universal meeting point specified above, however, he deserves, has earned and achieved, expects no more no less than, the same kind of treatment you do, I do, that any of us do. We may not be *equal* to him but he is of the same imprint, membership in the same race and plainly and simply deserves the kind of treatment, respect, affection one to another, that such status deserves.

We are of the *same sameness*. We are of the *same different difference*. If that doesn't earn us some sort of straight across the boards accepting membership in the same club I can't envision anything that ever will. Certainly striving to be the *equal* of somebody will never do it.

So, in that definition and determination of what profit means, what kind of profit is part of your plan for the company? Does it really include all employees? Does it give them a feeling of ownership, of participation, of inclusion, a piece of the territory?

That consideration of profit and its resultant definition could almost by itself work some sort of miracle in our communicating process. People hear extremely well when it affects their personal well being, status, welfare. They hear positively what is going to be of use to them. They hear negatively what isn't. They react accordingly.

As a suggestion then, if you start with a definition of what profit is, its implication and meaning, the lines of determining what needs to be done to acheve it will be well drawn and defined.

At that point, which of these objectives can be realistically achieved? Not by capitalization, production, plans, personnel, programming or promotion, but rather by what means of the communicating art or discipline are you going to accomplish those goals? No communication—no production for example. No communication—no financing, to draw another ultimate.

Business philosophers and others like to talk about the big picture, particularly for public consumption. The average employee, should he by chance audit one of those speeches by his boss would be in for a surprise. He has never heard those plans expressed in that way before. He doesn't necessarily need to feel too put upon. Might even surprise some of the vice presidents!

For consideration for the next step, how about letting the outfit know what the company plans to do, how it thinks it can be done, what the role of each department and its personnel is, what profits and for whom may be achieved, what the accomplishment will mean for all concerned?

This takes for granted that in the communicating planning stage you have sought and received information, facts, ideas and suggestions from that same total encompassment of personnel; have evaluated it and put that of it to work which seems practicable; after first presentation have left room for suggested addition, subtraction and revision before final and formal implementation; are playing it loose and flexible thereafter to allow for emergencies, exigencies and contingencies which are sure to develop; and, lastly that you not only have a hot communicating line that is busy and open but operating effectively with as little breakdown as possible.

To manage this continuum of communicating effectiveness, the following are some factors for consideration.

1. If possible, meetings of *all* company personnel, oftener. The retail business is particularly adept and competent at sales meetings for all employees prior to a special event.

2. Department meetings, from chairman of the boardship to line personnel, oftener.

3. Training, orientation, instruction and information meetings, oftener.

One of the biggest complaints of business is that it is *meetinged* to death, that there isn't enough time for personnel to do their work let alone attend meetings. Isn't it just possible that what is being communicated at those meetings needs a good look in terms of what is being communicated, how it is being communicated, by whom, how effectively, to what audience, for what purpose, how well it works and what is its payoff—if any?

The oftenness of such meetings is not necessarily the criterion. There is a strong possibility that somebody decided to hold a meeting for whatever panic button reason of the moment. He did, got on the horse, galloped off in all directions at once, without firing a shot—that hit anything.

EDUCATION, TRAINING AND INSTRUCTION

There is a widely developing need on the broad communicating front in education, training and instruction. Even the academicians have been faced with not only an educational explosion in needs and numbers but with the plain necessity of making what they are teaching more meaningful and more inclusive of a range of practicable subject material.

Paralleling that development is a similarly exploding need for away from the company, in company and on the job educating processes. This need may be accomplished through: companies themselves with some kind of training division; courses in extended education of varying degree and effectiveness conducted by universities, colleges and technical and vocational schools; and specialists from associations and professions, arts and crafts who conduct seminars, courses and conference.

Business and industry finds itself harder and harder pressed to find specially trained and educated personnel who qualify for what can probably best be described as *disciplines* in this very fast-breaking, complexing, overnight developing age of specialized functions. As an observation, I submit that colleges and universities, traditionally rooted in the academic concept, have found it impossible, or at the very least, difficult, to first of all develop applicable curriculi, valid subject matter and instructors, and, second—granting the first to be possible—find themselves extremely loath to include what they consider to be vocational training in that upper register labelled *academic*, and therefore accredited.

Vocational and technical schools, on the other hand, stay so close to actual and applied job skills and training, that they can't envision the need or market for (or haven't learned yet how to meet it) this gap area I am suggesting as *disciplines* for business and industry. Neither of the two teaching institutions and means—academic and vocational—have managed to meet this unfulfilled void with much other than a garden sprinkling can, when what is needed is an entire watering system.

The academic system basically prepares us for professions. Vocational education basically prepares us for jobs. Between the two areas is neither profession nor job, but a wide and ever increasing range of *disciplines*. Communicator is one, for example. Director of training is another. Corporate safety director or supervisor is still another. Supervisor or foreman as such, management and administrative personnel. Policemen. Driver education teachers. To name some.

I suggest that the gap area which I have outlined could be called something like, Institute For Practical and Applied Disciplines for Business and Industry. Preferably at the university or college level, its curriculi could become accredited, (if desirable) and instructors could also be accredited out of experience and ability in that discipline without necessity, necessarily, for degree and qualification via the traditional academic route.

In this case I would like to see the traditional emphasis reversed. Experience in the discipline, however finally specified, to be the principal and basic qualifying factor—and the degree neither helping, hindering or required.

You can be certain that specialized curriculum or general curriculi in this discipline area will originate from business and industry, by those who cope first-hand, bread and butter, day by day, with the problem; and that instructors to teach the discipline would originate from that same level, with qualifying training and instruction for the position from their own peer group within those discipline fields.

I submit to this readership on an individual profit and achievement basis first, that there is an urgent need for capable communicators, and—qualified at this point as best you can, by whatever means you can imaginatively and creatively put together, seek out and study, by application and in some ways by simple dint of doing until a better method comes along—that you can personally carve out a career for yourself that is interesting, consuming and profitable.

I suggest also, that decision makers in business and industry face this problem head on and decide that there is a need and a place for a communicator (whatever you decide to call him) at your right or left hand, whose responsibility, department and function, is to translate into effective communicating terms those goals, objectives and functions essential to business and its profit.

As a matter of simple fact, without any qualification whatsoever, effective communication is in some ways our least understood, most *unemployed resource*. It is also, as much as we pay homage to it on the one hand and ignore it on the other, the only real means available to accomplish anything we set out to do.

Communication unemployment we tolerate at our peril. "Every man a Communicator" is the modern paraphrase of Kingfish Huey Long. We shouldn't fail for lack of trying. Let us praise real communicators in public places. Let us send rescue missions for those down in the wild. They're needed. Are they ever needed! To meet the need, let's become Communicators ourselves.

Daniel Boone: "I was never lost, but once I was confused for three days."

VIGNETTE

HE HAD BEEN ALONE. One against the elements many times in his life.

A dim light in the cockpit. A star to navigate by. A last fuel tank to cut in before landfall. A landfall out of reach should the switchover fail. Four times he cut that tank in. Four times it failed. The fifth time the engine sputtered, then caught and ran.

He had lived through the loneliest time of all. Man against nature in a fight for his life. Fuel line busted. Aircraft down in the most remote back country in the world. The pitiful supply of food on hand when he cracked up—an orange, some chocolate candy bars—gone. Nothing to go on but hope, guts, backbone, courage, determination, some tears and an infinitely indomitable spirit.

Ticker tape parades. Fame. Adulation. Those were the in-between times when the fear and the loneliness faded into the background. Forgotten, but not gone.

"Hell," the air hero said, "In those days if I didn't get a 'piece' every half hour—I got a headache."

"Of the action," air hero no doubt intends to add. Is air hero the finally lost non-communicator or the crash-landed communicator? Time will do her business and show the answer. If the air hero is a downed communicator, he'll build a communication raft of neatly glued-together words and quickly be heard again. He'll return, if not on a wing and a prayer, on a strong conviction and a neat argument. Possibly with a slight limp. And he'll be more than welcome. He'll be essential.

Postscript

So what else is new?

Not much really, since *Pithecanthropus Erectus* first had to defend and fend for himself against all comers, standing at the entrance to his cave, growling ferociously and vigorously brandishing the jawbone of an ass.

He was a *total* communicator at that point, with one, single, simple, fully transmitted and understood, intent, purpose, function and objective. Survival. Standing up to a threatened incursion of, what Robert Ardrey has aptly described as his *territorial imperative*. Willing to defend it with his life, if necessary, and just as single purposed in keeping his own life by taking that of the aggressor as a far more satisfactory arrangement for him.

The circumstance has altered but the situation has not. He is once again at that same threshold he has had to guard so frequently in the past. I submit, if we really listen carefully, he is in the same murderous frame of mind.

Prophet me no profits and pooh pooh me no excrement in any palliative, excusatory, rationalistic apologia in explanation of the system and its need for perpetuation. While we're at it—*stop right there*. Don't accuse me of being anti-system, anti-establishment or antidisestablishmentarianism.

I can explain the system, its validity, its purpose, its achievement and its faults as well as the next. I am part of it, had something to do with its establishment, make no apology for it, and think it is the best system extant.

It is simply due for, experiencing and undergoing, some *change*. *Change* is painful. *Change* is difficult to achieve. We are inclined to stay in an uncomfortable, uninhabitable rut rather than change to something new. We would rather be comfortable in our accustomed uncomfortableness than uncomfortable in an unaccustomed uncomfortableness. "Don't rock the boat, baby, it makes waves."

Change, like death however, is inevitable. Sometimes lack of change can be a kind of death of its own. We need to pause and consider what the world we live in is really like today. It is miraculous, marvellous, magnificent—and magnified. Moon-magnified if you will, to use a kind of crystallizing symbol.

As a fleeting, passing thought, it is in a way as if all the communicating faculties and facilities we have mustered, mounted and managed, are that *spirit* and *soul* we talk so glibly about, reflecting through those eyes the middling, muddling and miserable subversion of that individual imprimatur, we have achieved.

There is a whole new future, challenge, opportunity and profit, stretching out before us. There always will be until the Apocalypse.

There is, that is, if we accept it for what it appears to be: a time for man to get a proper perspective on that *mechanism* and its position of helper, not manipulator or manager of mankind; a time to recognize that man's rebellion, evidenced in so many ways, has a legitimate, valid and just cause—to him. The overrun of him as an individual, a violation that not only can but will be determined by a majority court of appeal; a time to begin to adjust those inequities, indignities, and inhumanities, in such a way that not only brings men directly face to face with one another, but makes it possible for man to face himself.

In some ways it is almost as simple in definition as that. *Making it possible for man to face himself.* In that inviolable spirit, soul, and individual imprimatur, there is an innate honesty about himself that man finds difficult to avoid, get around, avert or ignore. That pesky rib again.

Who makes it possible for man to face himself?

Not the experts or expertise. Not the smoke screening dissembling dialectic of the fast encroaching Society of the Saviours of the World. (And that's a big one Brother, with an exploding membership on both sides of the fence, establishment and antiestablishment.) Not the programs that promise, guarantee and give us everything from birth to death—except immortality, but really give us nothing, no way to earn and work for our own individual self-respect. Not the pat-'em-on-the-popo-send-'em-away-with-a-sucker-while-I-secure-the-monopoly-on-sugar psychology.

No sir! *It's you and me buddy.* It has never been any different. It never will be. You and me, that is, as long as we don't fall into the same gilt edged trap, the first gleam and glitter of which appears on the far off horizon the first time any of us experiences that feeling of influence, power and control over others. That's a sunrise that even the best-intentioned as well as the worst-intentioned amongst us, basks in the rays and warmth of. For awhile. Sometimes for a long time.

We might as well, while we are at it, set off another giant four-incher on this glorious 4th of July. Any and every dissident, rebel, anarchist, nihilist, power-centrist, expert, programmer, planner, leader, politician or profiteer, has the same problem. Interesting, isn't it, to consider us all in the same boat? Not only interesting, but overlooked, unrecognized, and certainly abhorrent as an idea if considered at all, by that fascinating mutuality of interest. Also true.

They not only have the same problem—they have the same enemy, or ally. The individual and his individuality.

It takes this fellow an unconscionably long time to get aroused. But that is his way, directly related to his unmatched, miraculous uniqueness. He has to get his toes stepped on to the point of breaking. He has to get badly bloodied and painfully bruised. He has to reach a point where his "territory" is not only threatened, but incursed. He has to sometimes see his fellows die defending something he doesn't understand yet. Then he moves, and even then I suggest, he moves with some hold back out of consideration for the other guy, until he becomes firmly convinced that the other guy has no consideration for him whatsoever.

Worthy of observation and record, although certainly bound to gain no popularity in some seats of wisdom and authority, is that all dissenting groups, no matter how valid, just or honorable their cause, fall heir to and are apt to be or are, guilty of the same charge and fallacy they ascribe to others.

They get caught up in a similar power-centrist, establishment mechanism of their own, with an apartheid and bigotry of its own, with a dialectic of its own, with actions, mannerisms, attitudes, customs and mores, that are just as anathemic, rejectable and unacceptable as the opposition.

He has come to the same cropper on the high road the other guy stumbled over on the low road.

I haven't, in my readily admitted amateur status, seen any of the current revolutions, that have a butter pat's chance in the red hot oven of a wood burning stove—of success. Unless they meet two classic requirements.

First, the individual imprimatur.

What they have left out, is the very basic factor in their own plea, logic, and reason for being—the denigration, degradation and dehumanization of the individual. Their own individuality is in it, but the individuality of others is not. That is, of course, a certainty on their side of the fence too. But individuality is a two edged sword, a many faceted weapon.

Second, the majority process.

So far, in this country at least, and those of the basic democratic tenet, any issue meets another test, a direct descendant of its forbear—the majority principle. The success of any rebellion, which may perforce initiate with a minority, is totally dependent upon its ability to secure a majority. That abilty must concede to, and operate on the principle of winning individuals one by one, adding up to a total number or group of sufficiently like intent, purpose and numbers, so that it becomes an identifiable, risking and acting majority who represent the biggest number for or against, and, therefore, any way you look at it, has the power edge.

This is a practical fact of life in these United States, willy nilly, like it or not, rage, rampage and roustabout as we will. It is, however, deeper than that. It is also an emotional fact of life, at the very wellspring of man's existence. Something that the democratic majority system has developed out of, or because of; something that man has lost sight of, lo these many times in all these many centuries; something he has eventually had to fight for (and will again), won, lost, got wiped out completely, then started all over again from scratch, waiting for that indestructible seed to sprout, flower and grow.

That—once again the nevermore in this thesis—is the inviolability of the individual imprimatur, the sheer genus of that wisdom of the universe which created man in that image, endowing him alone of all its creatures with the challenge, the opportunity, the problem, and the decision, of managing his own destiny. For in simple fact if he does not, somebody will.

Whoever does not believe it is a fool. Whoever rails against it is a false prophet. Whoever lives by such false premise shall also die by it. It may take a long time, but die by it he will, or the universe as we know it will.

How does this all relate to communication? *It is communication.* It starts or ends there. It functions or malfunctions there. It continues or discontinues there. It succeeds or fails there.